STRATEGIES FOR TEACHING
Prekindergarten Music

MENC wishes to thank
Carolynn A. Lindeman, for developing and coordinating this series;
Wendy Sims and the associate editors for selecting,
writing, and editing the strategies
for this book;
and the following teachers for submitting strategies:

Frances W. Aronoff

Peggy D. Bennett

Elaine D. Bernstorf

Beverly Brook

Stephanie K. Burton

Cynthia Colwell

Barbara H. Cory

Lori Custodero

Sandra J. Denmead

John M. Feierabend

Martha Giles

Catherine Jarjisian

Dale Ludwig

Pamela S. Moore

Rachel Nardo

Diane Persellin

Phyllis Relyea

Mary Lou Van Rysselberghe

Bettina Schwartz

Marcelyn Smale

Susan Tarnowski

STRATEGIES FOR TEACHING

Prekindergarten Music

Compiled and edited by
Wendy L. Sims

Associate Editors
Jane W. Cassidy, Amy Freshwater, and C. Dianne Mack

MENC: THE NATIONAL ASSOCIATION FOR MUSIC EDUCATION

YOUR KEY TO IMPLEMENTING THE NATIONAL STANDARDS FOR MUSIC EDUCATION

MENC MENC
MENC MENC

CONTENTS

PREFACE

The Music Educators National Conference (MENC) created the *Strategies for Teaching* series to help preservice and inservice music educators implement the K–12 National Standards for Music Education and the MENC Prekindergarten Standards. To address the many components of the school music curriculum, each book in the series focuses on a specific curricular area and a particular level. The result is eleven books spanning the K–12 areas of band, chorus, general music, strings/orchestra, guitar, keyboard, and specialized ensembles. A prekindergarten book and a guide for college music methods classes complete the series.

The purpose of the series is to seize the opportunity presented by the landmark education legislation of 1994. With the passage of the Goals 2000: Educate America Act, the arts were established for the first time in our country's history as a core, challenging subject in which all students need to demonstrate competence. Voluntary academic standards were called for in all nine of the identified core subjects—standards specifying what students need to know and be able to do when they exit grades 4, 8, and 12.

In music, content and achievement standards were drafted by an MENC task force. They were examined and commented on by music teachers across the country, and the task force reviewed their comments and refined the standards. While all students in grades K–8 are expected to meet the achievement standards specified for those levels, two levels of achievement—proficient and advanced—are designated for students in grades 9–12. Students who elect music courses for one to two years beyond grade 8 are expected to perform at the proficient level. Students who elect music courses for three to four years beyond grade 8 are expected to perform at the advanced level.

The music standards, together with the dance, theatre, and visual arts standards, were presented in final form—*National Standards for Arts Education*—to the U.S. Secretary of Education in March 1994. Recognizing the importance of early childhood education, MENC went beyond the K–12 standards and established content and achievement standards for the prekindergarten level as well, which are included in MENC's *The School Music Program: A New Vision*.

Now the challenge at hand is to implement the standards at the state and local levels. Implementation may require schools to expand the resources necessary to achieve the standards as specified in MENC's *Opportunity-to-Learn Standards for Music Instruction: Grades PreK–12*. Teachers will need to examine their curricula to determine if they lead to achievement of the standards. For many, the standards reflect exactly what has always been included in the school music curriculum—they represent best practice. For others, the standards may call for some curricular expansion.

To assist in the implementation process, this series offers teaching strategies illustrating how the music standards can be put into action in the music classroom. The strategies themselves do not suggest a curriculum. That, of course, is the responsibility of school districts and individual teachers. The strategies, however, are designed to help in curriculum development, lesson planning, and assessment of music learning.

The teaching strategies are based on the content and achievement standards specified in the *National Standards for Arts Education* (K–12) and *The School Music Program: A New Vision* (PreK–12). Although the strategies, like the standards, are designed primarily for four-year-olds, fourth graders, eighth graders, and high school seniors, many may be developmentally appropriate for students in other grades. Each strategy, a lesson appropriate for a portion of a class session or a complete class session, includes an objective (a clear statement of what the student will be able to do), a list of necessary materials, a description of what prior student learning and experiences are expected, a set of procedures, and the indicators of success. A follow-up section identifies ways learning may be expanded.

The *Guide for Music Methods Classes* contains strategies appropriate for preservice instructional settings in choral, instrumental, and general music methods classes. The teaching strategies in this Guide relate to the other books in the series and reflect a variety of teaching/learning styles.

Bringing a series of thirteen books from vision to reality in a little over a year's time required tremendous commitment from many, many music educators—not to mention the tireless help of the MENC publications staff. Literally hundreds of music teachers across the country answered the call to participate in this project, the largest such participation in an MENC publishing endeavor. The contributions of these teachers and the books' editors are proudly presented in the various publications.

—*Carolynn A. Lindeman*
Series Editor

---

*Carolynn A. Lindeman, professor of music at San Francisco State University, served on the MENC task force that developed the music education standards. She is the author of three college textbooks (*The Musical Classroom, PianoLab, *and* MusicLab) *and numerous articles.*

INTRODUCTION

Music is a very natural, joyful part of young children's lives. Children's musical behaviors often are spontaneous: humming to themselves while sitting in the shopping cart, requesting a favorite lullaby recording at bedtime, chanting the traditional "Nah-nah-nah-nah-nah" on the playground, singing a song they have just learned for anyone who will listen, making a drum from an empty oatmeal box and a wooden spoon, or dancing to music that is played in their home. One needs only to observe children—at play, watching television, listening to the car radio, or going about their daily routine—to find many more examples of young children's self-directed musical activity.

Music experiences planned and guided by teachers, caregivers, and parents also play an important role in young children's musical development. By facilitating activities such as learning new songs, rhymes, and fingerplays during group time in a prekindergarten setting; setting up a music corner in the classroom where children work in small groups exploring various sound sources; suggesting that children paint a picture to illustrate a favorite song; or taking children to family concerts in the local park, school, or shopping mall, adults can provide experiences that capitalize on young children's enthusiastic responses to music. Adults can also open up new musical horizons for children.

All of these experiences help provide a foundation for young children's future music learning. As children sing, move, listen, play, and create, whether on their own, with other children, or with nurturing adults, they begin to form concepts about characteristics of music, its expressive qualities, and its role in people's lives. High-quality, positive interactions with music during the early years can provide the basis for music as a source of pleasure and creative expression throughout life.

Developmentally Appropriate Curriculum

Young children learn by interacting directly with the subject matter. A developmentally appropriate music curriculum for young children must be highly experiential and hands-on, providing many opportunities for children to make and respond to music. While four-year-olds have begun to build a vocabulary of terms and expressions to describe music, these words are only meaningful when drawn from and connected directly to the children's experiences.

The activities presented in this book are designed to engage children actively in experiences that will lead them to draw conclusions about and make connections among the materials presented. Many of the procedures include opportunities for the children to help guide the direction of the activity, provide creative input, and contribute their own ideas. By following the children's lead and demonstrating that they value the children's creativity and efforts, teachers can help children personalize the learning experience while developing the children's self-confidence and leadership skills.

Teachers of young children must recognize that there will be a relatively wide range of individual differences, perhaps more so than in any other stage of children's development. For example, while some four-year-olds can sing familiar songs using accurate pitches, others can only approximate the song, incorporating the general contour (rise and fall) of the melody. A number of children may be able to match and maintain a steady beat, while others find this a difficult task. Many children join into new activities eagerly, while a few feel more secure after they've watched other children participate. Labeling children "poor singers," requiring them to drill or practice tasks repetitively, entreating them to "try harder," or nagging at them to "join in" are all counterproductive teacher behaviors.

As a result of many positive experiences and gentle encouragement in safe and comfortable environments, most children will eventually catch up with their peers by age five or six without additional adult intervention. While "indicators of success" are included for each teaching strategy in this book, the teacher must ultimately decide the appropriate level of achievement to expect from each child.

The prekindergarten standards and teaching strategies provided here are aimed at four-year-olds. In settings where children are placed in mixed age groupings, or for use with groups of younger children, adaptations should be made and expectations adjusted accordingly. Although specific prior experiences are indicated for many of the strategies, all standards will be achieved most readily if the children have been exposed to music as a regular part of their home and/or classroom environment throughout their early years.

Organizing Classroom Music Experiences

Music should be included within prekindergarten childcare/preschool settings in several ways. Time should be set aside regularly for large- and small-group music activities, and for individual interaction with musical materials. Many of the procedures described in this book may be adapted for use in any one of these settings.

Music making throughout one's lifespan is often a social and collaborative activity. A special energy is created when people listen to music together, whether by sharing a special recording with friends or joining members of large concert audiences. Also, the experience of creating and performing together, with each individual contributing as a valuable group member, sets music apart from many other areas of study. Adults generally don't participate in group algebra or group chemistry or group history, but most will participate in group music making or listening, whether by singing "The Star Spangled Banner" together at a sporting event, participating in a community music group, listening to the organist at a wedding, or attending concerts, ballet, and musical theater. Large-group music activities within a flexible, child-centered environment provide an important component of young children's musical experiences.

While large-group music experiences are valuable in many respects, they do have the drawback of creating a situation that may be distracting for young children: it may be difficult for children to hear their own voices or for each to have a turn trying out their own ideas or participating in a discussion. Therefore, young children also need time to interact with music individually or in small groups. More intimate settings allow children to concentrate more intently on individual sounds and on their own voice, to experiment more freely with their ideas, and to have more sustained dialogue about music than is possible in a large group. In a prekindergarten classroom setting, small-group or one-on-one experiences are often structured as one of a variety of activities, or centers, from which children may choose or among which they rotate during free-choice times or at designated times in the class schedule.

In addition to adult-organized encounters with music, child-initiated music activities form another context in which valuable learning takes place. Children often chant, sing, or move rhythmically while playing, or they may choose a recording or describe a musical experience for class "sharing time." They may accompany activities with appropriate sounds: cooing for a baby doll, saying "whee" with a rising or falling pitch while running through a sprinkler, making truck noises when playing imaginatively with blocks. Generally, adults should make note of the children's spontaneous music making and sound exploration, perhaps to draw upon later in classroom activities, but should avoid intervening and "taking over" the child-directed play environment.

Integrating Music into the PreK Curriculum

The world as perceived by young children is not divided into discrete content areas. Separating content into "music," or "science," or "language arts," or "life skills" is an adult-constructed paradigm; it has been deconstructed recently by professionals in early childhood education. While goals for each content area may remain intact, learning activities are often designed to accomplish a variety of interrelated objectives.

Balancing the integrity of each discipline within the interrelatedness of the curriculum presents a challenge for teachers, particularly with respect to music. Music is a very powerful medium for instruction. Music activities are highly motivating for most children, and music can be used to help create a pleasant classroom environment. Singing games and activities may capture and maintain children's attention for longer periods of time than talking-based activities. For these reasons, music activities may be used in a variety of ways to help children meet the objectives of many areas of the curriculum. To the extent that this use increases children's opportunities to interact with quality musical materials, this provides an excellent way for children to meet music education objectives as well.

A problem arises, however, when music becomes merely a tool with which to implement other aspects of the curriculum. This happens when musical materials are chosen not for their musical quality, but for their relation to the subject matter under consideration. Merely singing topical songs or playing a piece during rest time with a title related to the unit of study is problematic if it is considered to be the day's contribution to the music curriculum. On the other hand, when activities are selected and used to meet objectives for both music and the integrated subject areas, each area of the curriculum will truly benefit from the others' contributions.

Although designed primarily to meet the musical goals represented by the standards, most of the strategies and materials presented in this book provide opportunities for developing these valuable curricular connections.

Using This Book

The teaching strategies provided in this book are designed to be accessible to teachers with various levels of music background. Ideally, every preschool or child-care center would employ a full-time staff member who is well-educated both in music and in early childhood development. This would provide for high-quality musical examples and experiences to be presented by a familiar adult, who is present to include music at opportune times throughout the day and to integrate it appropriately across the curriculum. When such a specialist is not employed as a staff member, MENC recommends that a music specialist with training in child development be employed to serve as a visiting teacher and consultant (*The School Music Program: A New Vision,* p. 10). Desirable characteristics for music teachers of young children are described in the "Position Statement on Early Childhood Education," adopted by the National Executive Board of the Music Educators National Conference in 1991 (used to guide the development of MENC's standards for the prekindergarten level; see page 89).

The strategies included in this book are presented as exemplars of materials and techniques for implementing an early childhood music curriculum designed to meet the content and achievement standards. They do not constitute a curriculum in and of themselves, however. Teachers must choose activities appropriate for their children, modify or adapt the activities as necessary, sequence them in a meaningful way, and evaluate their effectiveness. Some of the standards may be met after using activities and materials from only three or four of the examples, while other standards may require many more than the five experiences provided to be mastered by the children. Teachers are encouraged to use the ideas presented here as springboards for their own creativity and as models for developing and implementing their own materials and activities.

The specific songs, rhymes, listening examples, and children's books included in the teaching strategies were selected based on their quality and age appropriateness, and because they represent a variety of genres and styles. An effort was made to use materials that could be obtained relatively easily. Most of the songs and rhymes appear frequently in song collections or methods texts, and most of the recordings and children's books are readily available in school and public libraries, at commercial book or music stores, or through educational catalogs. The sources of materials indicated within the teaching examples do not comprise an exhaustive list; many of the materials may be found in several different publications. Substitution of comparable examples from the teacher's personal repertoire and collection of materials is encouraged.

While the strategies employed in this book present models of good practice, this material is not intended, nor sufficient, to constitute a teaching methods text. The material in this book should be used in conjunction with the information and research base presented in early childhood music methods books, including characteristics of young children's musical development, effective teaching methodologies and practices, quality musical materials, curriculum development, adaptations for children with special needs, and appropriate assessment and evaluation techniques (for example, MENC's 1993 publication, *Music in Prekindergarten: Planning and Teaching*).

Conclusion

One of the nation's educational goals for the year 2000 is that all children will begin school ready to learn. MENC's standards for music in prekindergarten are designed to help achieve this goal by defining what children should know and be able to do with respect to music when they enter kindergarten. As the first arts education organization to generate and endorse standards for the prekindergarten level, MENC has taken a leadership position in acknowledging the importance of arts education in early childhood. It is now the responsibility of individual music educators, early childhood educators, and parents to work together to meet the challenge of ensuring that all young children have the opportunity to participate in high-quality, developmentally appropriate music activities and experiences. By achieving these standards, children will be well on their way to acquiring the knowledge, skills, and attitudes that will prepare them to derive fulfillment from music throughout the rest of their lives.

STRATEGIES

STANDARD 1A

Singing and playing instruments: Children use their
voices expressively as they speak, chant, and sing.

Objective

- Children will use their voices expressively by singing, speaking, shouting, and whispering.

Materials

- Nursery rhymes, such as "Hickory Dickory Dock" in *Go in and out the Window* by Dan Fox (New York: Metropolitan Museum of Art/Henry Holt, 1987)

Prior Knowledge and Experiences

- Children are familiar with speaking and singing the nursery rhyme.

Procedures

1. Chant the nursery rhyme together. Identify this as using a "speaking" voice.

2. Sing the nursery rhyme together. Identify this as using a "singing" voice.

3. Ask the children to create a hand gesture to symbolize their speaking voice and another to symbolize their singing voice (for example, singing might be symbolized by hands gliding smoothly in the air, or by conducting gestures, while speaking might be symbolized by hands opening and closing in imitation of a mouth).

4. Ask the children to follow your hands while performing the rhyme. Perform it twice in a row, the first time using the singing gesture, switching to the speaking gesture for the second.

5. In a whispering voice, ask the children what a mouse would sound like if it were trying to talk to another mouse while sneaking around the house. Identify this as a "whispering" voice. Whisper the rhyme together. Ask the children to create a hand gesture to symbolize their whispering voice to accompany the rhyme (for example, holding an index finger in front of the lips). Perform the rhyme together three times, first singing, then speaking; then adding the whispering voice and gesture.

6. Ask a child to demonstrate how a mouse would call out to another mouse across a field. Be sure that this "shouting" voice is not too loud or harsh. Ask the children to create a hand gesture to symbolize their shouting voice to accompany the rhyme (for example, cupping the hands around the mouth like a megaphone). Perform the rhyme four times, adding the shouting voice and gesture.

7. Using the gestures as signals, vary the order of the voices used to recite the rhyme. Have children take turns being the leaders. (For singing versions, be sure to start the song with the children so they have a model to help them find a common pitch.)

Indicators of Success

- Children demonstrate singing, speaking, whispering, and shouting voices when prompted by gestures or words.

Follow-up

- Use the gestures created to guide the performance of different rhymes (for example, "Little Boy Blue," "I'm a Little Teapot").
- Add other types of voices the children may suggest.

Singing and playing instruments: Children use their voices expressively as they speak, chant, and sing.

Objective

- Children will be able to use their head voice expressively while speaking.

Materials

- *The Gingerbread Man* by Paul Galdone (New York: Seabury Press, 1975)

Prior Knowledge and Experiences

- Children have made head-voice sounds (light, higher than speaking pitch, sing-song type sounds) through participation in voice exploration activities such as siren sounds, ghost sounds, owl sounds, imitating slide whistle sounds, or using the voice to "follow" wavy lines or shapes.

Procedures

1. Perform the couplet spoken by the gingerbread man, modeling an appropriately expressive head-voice sound ("Run, run, as fast as you can; You can't catch me, I'm the gingerbread man").

2. Invite the children to echo-speak the couplet, one phrase at a time, until they can speak the whole couplet using their head voice in an appropriately expressive manner.

3. Read the story with the children; have them speak the couplet in the appropriate places.

Indicators of Success

- Children use their head voice expressively while speaking.

Follow-up

- Contrast head voices with chest voices (heavy, speaking-voice pitch level) to dramatize characters in different stories (for example, in "Three Little Pigs," speak the pigs' dialogue in head voice and the wolf's words in chest voice).

Singing and playing instruments: Children use their voices expressively as they speak, chant, and sing.

Objective

- Children will use their voices flexibly and expressively to portray different characters, shifting among different voices on cue.

Materials

- Favorite short poems, such as "Signals" or "Crowded Tub" from *A Light in the Attic* by Shel Silverstein (New York: Harper & Row, 1981)
- Two puppets representing characters with contrasting voices

Prior Knowledge and Experiences

- Children have learned to speak the poem and have experienced it in different contexts (for example, speaking rhythmically while keeping a beat, dramatizing with movement).

Procedures

1. Review the poem to ensure that children know it well and can speak it in unison.

2. Introduce the puppets, asking questions about the kinds of voices they would have, especially in relation to each other. (If available puppets do not present an obvious contrast, each can "prefer" a particular type of voice.) The children should experiment with providing voices for the puppets and decide on a voice for each puppet to use for this activity.

3. Ask the children to say the poem using the voice of the puppet that is held up. Perform the poem in its entirety twice, first using one puppet, then the other.

4. Challenge the children to follow the puppets again, to "watch closely because they might try to fool you." Begin the poem with one puppet; halfway through, switch puppets. When children are following easily by changing their voices accordingly, switch more frequently, until they can follow switches occurring at any phrase.

5. Provide the opportunity for pairs of children to perform the rhyme, one child for each puppet, using whichever voice each chooses.

Indicators of Success

- Children create a variety of expressive voices and shift among them with ease.

Follow-up

- Place puppets where they will be available for students to use in a similar manner during free play time.
- Repeat the group activity with different pairs of puppets, different types of voices, and different poems and rhymes.

Singing and playing instruments: Children use their voices expressively as they speak, chant, and sing.

Objective

- Children will use their voices to approximate ascending and descending pitches.

Materials

- Nursery rhymes with texts that imply ascending and descending actions, for example, "Jack and Jill," and "Humpty Dumpty"

Prior Knowledge and Experiences

- Children know the rhymes well and can speak them together.

Procedures

1. Recite "Jack and Jill" for the children. Elongate the vowel sound of the word "up," speaking it with a long, ascending glissando (sliding the voice without separating the pitches). Use a descending glissando for the word "down." Accompany the words with hand gestures to show the pitch levels.

2. Invite the children to imitate the sounds and motions for "up" and "down." Speak the rhyme together, adding the sounds and motions.

3. Chant "Humpty Dumpty" as a group. Ask the children to find a word in the rhyme where Humpty gets higher or gets lower. They discover that the word "fall" is a downward motion and use their voices and hands to show this when speaking the rhyme again. Try other suggestions that they might have, such as using voices to show Humpty climbing up to sit on the wall. (Remember, children may have many answers that are as "right" to their way of thinking as the one you were thinking of from an adult perspective.)

Indicators of Success

- Children demonstrate their voices getting higher or getting lower.
- Children notice words in other stories and rhymes that indicate directionality and demonstrate the direction with their voices.

Follow-up

- Present the children with an action that is both ascending and descending, such as "over" in "Jack Be Nimble" or "Hey Diddle, Diddle." Use the voice to demonstrate an archlike shape, connecting ascending and descending pitches smoothly.

- Read the picture book *Mortimer* by Robert Munsch (Toronto: Annick Press, 1985), inviting the children to join in every time a family member climbs up and down the stairs by speaking the five "thumps" with the appropriate pitch direction.

Singing and playing instruments: Children use their voices expressively as they speak, chant, and sing.

Objective

- Children will use dynamics and tempo expressively when singing.

Materials

- Lullaby, such as "All Night, All Day" in *150 American Folk Songs* edited by Peter Erdei (New York: Boosey & Hawkes, 1974)

Prior Knowledge and Experiences

- Children have learned to sing the song.

Procedures

1. Have the children sing the song. Review its purpose (a song to put a baby to sleep, called a lullaby).

2. Lead a discussion about how the song should be sung so that it will help the baby fall asleep, not keep the baby awake. Try out and discuss children's suggestions. (Most groups of children will decide that the song should be soft. Some may also decide that it should be slow.)

3. Ask the children to sing the song three times in a row, getting softer and softer each time until the baby is asleep.

4. Ask the children to sing the song three times in a row while pretending to hold and rock a baby, rocking and singing slower and slower each time until the baby is asleep.

Indicators of Success

- Children demonstrate changes in dynamic levels or tempos while singing familiar songs.

Follow-up

- Try changing both the dynamics and tempo at the same time. While the children should be able to do this when imitating the teacher, it will be difficult for most of the children to do this independently.

- Experiment with other songs that imply changing dynamics or tempos.

- Dramatize the song by having half the class sing to the other half, until the second half "falls asleep," or by having the children "sing the teacher to sleep."

STANDARD 1B

Singing and playing instruments: Children sing a variety of simple songs in various keys, meters, and genres, alone and with a group, becoming increasingly accurate in rhythm and pitch.

Objective

- Children will sing individual responses in the context of a question-and-answer song.

Materials

- "Going on a Picnic" by Lynn Freeman Olson in *The Music Connection,* Grade K (Morristown, NJ: Silver Burdett Ginn, 1995)
- Picnic basket or sack containing eight real or pretend picnic items (for example, sandwich, apple, cookie, tablecloth, soccer ball)

Prior Knowledge and Experiences

- Children have experience with question-and-answer rhymes and songs.

Procedures

1. Sing the refrain section of the song ("Going on a picnic. . ."), patting knees with hands to the beat to represent "footsteps."

2. Bring out the picnic basket and remove items one at a time, handing each item to a child while singing about it during the question-and-answer section of the song. Example: Teacher sings, "Did you bring the sandwich?" Group responds, with teacher assistance as long as necessary, "Yes, I brought the sandwich." Continue until all items are distributed and the children are comfortable singing the answers.

3. Repeat the refrain and continue on to the question-and-answer section. Sing the question, making eye contact with the child holding the object, and invite the child to sing the answer as a solo. Repeat refrain until all items are accounted for.

4. Repeat the activity as necessary, allowing children to share items, until everyone who would like a chance to sing has had a turn.

Indicators of Success

- Children sing their part at the correct time within the question-and-answer format.

Follow-up

- Sing the song without the props. The teacher may sing the question using a child's name ("Sandy, what will you bring?"), and the child responds with an object he or she chooses ("I'll bring hot dogs"). Another variation is to have everyone "bring" a classmate. The teacher sings the question "Chris, who will you bring?" and Chris sings the name of another child ("I'll bring Jamie"). The teacher sings the question to Jamie, who chooses another child, and so on.

- Sing the song when actually preparing for a school picnic or a different event (for example, going to a ball game).

Singing and playing instruments: Children sing a variety of simple songs in various keys, meters, and genres, alone and with a group, becoming increasingly accurate in rhythm and pitch.

Objective

- Children will sing songs in echo style and insert their own ideas into the lyrics of a song.

Materials

- "Down by the Bay" in *Music for Little People* by John Feierabend (New York: Boosey & Hawkes, 1989) and *Music: A Way of Life for the Young Child,* 3d ed., by Kathleen Bayless and Marjorie Ramsey (Columbus, OH: Merrill, 1987)

Prior Knowledge and Experiences

- Children have experience with echo singing.

Procedures

1. Present the song "Down by the Bay," with children echoing each phrase of the first section, the teacher singing the punch line "Did you ever see a moose. . . ," and all finishing with "down by the bay."

2. Sing the song several times with different punch lines. For example: "Did you ever see a goat, rowing a boat?" "Did you ever see some llamas, wearing pajamas?" Help the children discover the rhyming words in the punch line.

3. Invite the children to think of other funny situations they could sing about for the punch line. Assist if necessary by providing the first part of the phrase using a word that is easy to rhyme. Example: "Did you ever see a cat (or snake, pig, bug, or other animal)?"

4. Ask the children to draw pictures of their ideas to be used the next time the song is sung.

5. When the children have their illustrations ready, sing the song, allowing individual children to sing their ideas while showing their pictures. Pictures may be hung around the room so children can sing each other's ideas as a group or during free choice time.

Indicators of Success

- Children echo-sing at the appropriate spots.
- Children insert their original ideas into the punch line of the song.

Follow-up

- Sing other echo-style and call-and-response songs (for example, "Charlie over the Ocean," "John the Rabbit").
- Provide additional opportunities for children to create their own lyrics for familiar songs or parts of songs.

Singing and playing instruments: Children sing a variety of simple songs in various keys, meters, and genres, alone and with a group, becoming increasingly accurate in rhythm and pitch.

Objective

- Children will use their voices freely and flexibly across their singing range.

Materials

- A variety of objects such as different types of balls, a feather, a scarf, etc.

Prior Knowledge and Experiences

- Children have experience using the words "high" and "low" to describe placement in space (for example, "That plane is flying way up high"; "I'm squatting down low").

Procedures

1. Hold a feather over your head. Ask if it is high or low. Hold the feather down by your feet and repeat the question.

2. Ask children to listen to the words you sing. Demonstrate by singing the word "high" on a high note when holding the feather up high, and the word "low" on a low note when holding the feather low.

3. Ask the children to join in (remind them to use singing voices that are light like the feather).

4. Have the children listen to the new way you will sing, following the feather. Hold the feather by the quill and gently move the feather up and down from high to low to high, following the movement with your voice by gliding up and down on the syllable "oo." Invite the children to join in. Hold the feather up high and drop it, following it with voices as it floats to the ground.

5. Use a ball and a scarf as stimuli for singing in a similar manner. Toss a ball up high and follow its upward and downward motion using the vowel "whee." Make various patterns in the air with the scarf and follow with the syllable "ah."

Indicators of Success

- Children use their voices freely to vocalize across their full range.

Follow-up

- Children may move the objects and take turns responding.
- Make scarves and feathers available to children to inspire vocal exploration during free play time.

Singing and playing instruments: Children sing a variety of simple songs in various keys, meters, and genres, alone and with a group, becoming increasingly accurate in rhythm and pitch.

Objective

- Children will demonstrate sustained interest in singing songs with many verses.

Materials

- Songs with many verses or with verses that may be repeated many times by adding new lyrics, such as "What Shall We Do When We All Go Out" in *American Folksongs for Children* by Ruth Crawford Seeger (Garden City, NY: Doubleday, 1980) and *The Music Connection*, Grade 1 (Morristown, NJ: Silver Burdett Ginn, 1995)

Prior Knowledge and Experiences

- Children have a repertoire of short songs acquired through daily singing in group time and at other times throughout the day.

Procedures

1. Ask the children to listen to the question they will hear in the song you are about to sing. Ask them to to think of an answer but to keep the answer inside their head until they are asked to share it (this will help keep eager children from calling out the answer and interrupting the song).

2. Sing the song "What Shall We Do" and ask if they have an answer inside their head. Call on one child who would like to share an answer, and then sing the song using the child's idea, making an attempt to use as many of the child's own words as can reasonably fit within the phrase of the song (for example, "Let's take a walk when we all go out" or "Let's swing on swings").

3. Continue with children's ideas for as long as most children are willing to participate. Using the children's ideas and giving all children a turn should stimulate sustained participation.

Indicators of Success

- Children sustain participation in songs for longer and longer periods of time, both with a group and individually.

- Children are eager to add words to create additional verses for songs and initiate this during other singing activities.

Follow-up

- Change the words of the song from "when we all go out" to "on a snowy day," "rainy day," and so on.

- Teach songs with many verses such as "This Old Man" by adding only one or two verses a day. Build the suspense and keep the children guessing what he will "play nicknack on" next. A picture book—for example, *This Old Man* by Carol Jones (Boston: Houghton Mifflin, 1990)—may help the children remember the words.

- Teach other songs for which new verses may be created.

- Provide picture books of songs with many verses in the reading corner or music center to help children remember the lyrics for individual singing.

- Sing songs with which a different motion may be used for each verse (for example, "Here We Go 'Round the Mulberry Bush").

Singing and playing instruments: Children sing a variety of simple songs in various keys, meters, and genres, alone and with a group, becoming increasingly accurate in rhythm and pitch.

Objective

- Children will identify songs in their repertoire and create songbooks to share their songs with family and friends.

Materials

- Paper and crayons, markers, or colored pencils

Prior Knowledge and Experiences

- Children have experience with illustrated songbooks containing familiar songs, such as *Go in and out the Window* by Dan Fox, (New York: Metropolitan Museum of Art/Henry Holt, 1987) and *Shake It to the One That You Love Best* by Cheryl Warren Mattox (El Sabrante, CA: Warren-Mattox Productions, 1989) and with some of the many picture books based on folksongs.

Procedures

1. With the children's help, make a list on a chart of many songs they know how to sing together. Help by humming bits of songs as hints if necessary. If one child volunteers a song you don't think the group knows how to sing, have the group try singing it, and have the children help evaluate whether they really know it or not.

2. Show the children a songbook with which they are familiar, and explain that everyone will be making a songbook.

3. Within the structure of a small-group activity, or with the assistance of parent or grandparent volunteers, review the song list with the children, and ask them each to choose a favorite to start their own songbook. Assure them that they will be able to choose more songs later (and/or on another day) to add to their book.

4. On the bottom of a plain piece of paper, print the name of the song the child has selected. Ask the child to sing the song and to draw a picture to show the song, so that he or she will be able to look at the picture and know which song it is.

5. Place the child's name on the finished picture; mention that you are saving the pictures until each child has enough to make a book.

6. Provide opportunities over a period of a few weeks for children to add songs to their book. Some children will want to include many songs; all children should be encouraged to include at least three or four. When the children are finished, they may make decorative covers, and the books may be stapled or pages punched and threaded with yarn.

7. Send home songbooks with a note to parents encouraging them to have the children show the pictures and sing the songs to family members and friends.

Indicators of Success

- Children identify songs they know and sing them for others.

Follow-up

- Have children to add to their songbooks at home or during free time.
- Provide a page for each verse of multiverse songs and have children each illustrate one verse to create a class book, or illustrate every verse to create their own song picture book.

Singing and playing instruments: Children experiment with a variety of instruments and other sound sources.

Objective

- Children will be able to select and play instruments and add movements to replace designated words in a familiar song.

Materials

- "She'll Be Comin' 'Round the Mountain" in *American Folksongs for Children* by Ruth Crawford Seeger (Garden City, NY: Doubleday, 1980)

- Poster with simple illustrations for each verse

- A variety of small percussion instruments, enough to allow for a unique sound for each verse

Prior Knowledge and Experiences

- Children have experience playing classroom percussion instruments.

- Children know the song "She'll Be Comin' 'Round the Mountain" with words and movements that occur at the end of phrases. (The poster will help children remember the sequence of verses.)

Procedures

1. Sing the song through, adding the words (spoken) and motions below at the end of each phrase (after the words "when she comes"). Children may refer to the poster to assist as necessary.

   - She'll be comin' 'round . . . ("Woo, woo"—pull chord like train whistle on each word)

   - She'll be driving six white horses . . . ("Whoa back"—pull reins back on each word)

   - We will all go out to meet her . . . ("Hi, friend"—wave hand once to right and to left)

   - We will all eat chicken and dumplings . . . ("Yum, yum"—rub tummy on each word)

2. Ask the children to sing the song again, this time not speaking the extra words but still performing the motions.

3. Ask individual children or pairs of children to choose an instrument to play for the spoken words associated with an assigned verse. Allow the children to practice playing their set of words (playing the instrument only two times and then stopping is difficult for some children).

4. Have children sing the song, with the group performing motions while each individual plays his or her instrument where the spoken words had been during the appropriate verse. Repeat to provide turns for all the children.

Indicators of Success

- Children choose an instrument and play it in the correct manner at the correct time in the music.

- Children perform the appropriate motions when singing the song.

Follow-up

- Add verses to the song.

- Chain the instruments and motions in reverse order (for verse one, use "woo woo"; for second verse, use "whoa back; woo, woo," and so on). A slower tempo and the poster will be essential for this step.

Singing and playing instruments: Children experiment with a variety of instruments and other sound sources.

Objective

- Children will find ways to make sound effects to enhance a story.

Materials

- A wide variety of sound sources, not necessarily instruments (there might be a box with everyday items with which children can make interesting sounds)

Prior Knowledge and Experiences

- Children have experiences with the sounds produced by available sound sources.

Procedures

1. Select an activity for dramatization; for example, taking a walk.

2. If possible, participate directly in the activity. For example, take a walk with the children around the neighborhood on a fall day. Notice and identify all the various sounds.

3. Back in the classroom the same day or the next, have children review sounds they heard and propose additional ones that might be heard under other conditions.

4. Have several children choose an instrument or sound source that best represents some of the sounds (for example, rustling paper for walking on leaves, paper cups for people walking, chime tree for the wind, glockenspiel for the sun, hand broom for walking in sand, lids to pots for thunder, voice for ocean waves, voice or whistling for birds, wooden train whistle for train, sand inside a plastic egg for a snake).

5. Space "sound" children throughout the room. Have remaining children play the role of going out for a walk.

6. Tell the story—in this case of children going out for a walk in the fall, perhaps starting out with the "walking" children pretending to put on their coats. When they walk near a "sound" child, cue that child to play his or her "instrument," and have the "walking" children pantomime the source of the sound (for example, raking the leaves, moving arms like branches of trees).

7. Have children switch roles and repeat, or create a new story using different sounds.

Indicators of Success

- Children identify appropriate sounds from different settings.
- Children are thoughtful and creative in selecting an instrument because it approximates some attribute of the original sound.
- Children play their "instruments" at appropriate times in the story.

Follow-up

- Change the story line, perhaps to represent a recent field trip, an imagined vacation, or a favorite book.

- Have different sound sources in the box—one time kitchen utensils, one time classroom utensils, one time musical instruments. Have children bring an item from home for the box.

- Have a child narrate a story while the others make sound effects.

- Read *The Listening Walk* by Paul Showers (New York: HarperTrophy, 1991), and compare the sounds heard in the story to the sounds heard on the class walk. Create sounds for those described in the book and add them to the story.

Singing and playing instruments: Children experiment with a variety of instruments and other sound sources.

Objectives

- Children will select sound sources to represent activities in a story.
- Children will play sound sources at dynamic levels and tempos appropriate to story line.
- Children will echo with expressive voices.

Materials

- Words to "Bear Hunt" in *Musical Games, Finger Plays, and Rhythmic Activities for Early Childhood* by Marian Wirth, Verna Stassevitch, Rita Shotwell, and Patricia Stemmler (West Nyack, NY: Parker, 1983) and *Share the Music,* Grade K, (New York: Macmillan/McGraw-Hill, 1995). The chanted story may also be improvised.
- A variety of sound sources

Prior Knowledge and Experiences

- Children have experience with sounds produced by available items, including body sounds.
- Children understand the concepts of fast/slow and loud/soft.

Procedures

1. Have children select sound sources for various portions of the story. Examples: opening door—ratchet or voice squeak; walking—rhythm sticks or hands patting thighs; wheat field—sandpaper blocks or rubbing hands together; bridge—tambourine or pounding fists on chest; tree—slide whistle or pantomime; river—guiro/other scraper for rowing a boat and/or sing "Row, Row"; tiptoe—fingers on table.

2. Practice making each sound slowly and quickly, and loudly and softly. Some children could make body sounds while others play instruments.

3. Start the "Bear Hunt," speaking very expressively as a model for the children to echo. As each place is encountered, the children should make the appropriate sounds. On the way to the cave, the tempo should be slow as if searching everywhere for the bear. On the way home from the cave, the tempo should be fast as if running away from the bear.

4. The number of "places" passed through on the way to the cave may be varied, but the places and sequence should be noted so that the children can be cued to recite the places in the reverse order "on the way home."

Indicators of Success

- Children identify sound sources that represent activities in the story.
- Children make sounds at appropriate volume and tempo levels in the story.
- Children speak expressively while echoing the chant.

Follow-up

- Do this activity while walking around the room. Have different stations to represent each of the places the children visit.
- At Halloween, pretend to be going though a haunted house with a ghost in the attic. Have children think of creepy and spooky noises they might hear in this house, then find sound sources to represent the sounds.

Singing and playing instruments: Children experiment with a variety of instruments and other sound sources.

Objective

- Children will explore the use of body sounds and their combinations to create a musical representation of sounds of nature.

Materials

- *Listen to the Rain* by Bill Martin Jr. (New York: Henry Holt, 1988)

Prior Knowledge and Experiences

- Children comprehend weather conditions related to a rain storm: wind, soft rain, hard rain, hail, thunder, hurricane, and so on.

- Children know several songs about rain, for example, "Rain, Rain, Go Away," "It's Raining, It's Pouring," "It Rained a Mist" in *Go in and out the Window* by Dan Fox (New York: Metropolitan Museum of Art/Henry Holt, 1987).

Procedures

1. Have children sit in circle. Sing rain songs and discuss different sounds that occur when it is raining. Read *Listen to the Rain* to stimulate more ideas about the sounds and sequence of a rainstorm. Find ways to use the body or voice to create the sounds.

2. Using sounds generated by the children, initiate a sound (for example, blowing air from mouth, rubbing palms together, patting thighs, stomping feet, snapping fingers, clapping hands); then point to students to copy in nonrhythmic manner.

3. Have children practice imitating the sounds, starting and stopping the sounds at your nonverbal cues.

4. Tell the children that they are going to create their own rainstorm. Demonstrate one sound, pointing to one child in the circle to copy, then add subsequent children, one at a time, until everyone is making sound. Stop the sound. Practice with other sounds until children can follow the nonverbal directions and understand that they will be brought in one at a time.

5. Decide what type of storm to create (spring rain, hurricane, thunderstorm). Start by having one child copy a sound, and go around the circle, adding one child at a time, until all are copying. Then change the sound, one child at a time, until all have changed, so sounds overlap. Continue with appropriate sequence of sounds. One sequence might be blowing air (wind), tapping two fingers into the opposite palm (light rain drops), patting thighs (heavy rain), occasional hand claps from individual children while other children continue patting (thunder), snapping, and blowing. Have one child at a time stop until the room is silent.

6. Record the piece and play it back while children close their eyes and imagine the rainstorm.

Indicators of Success

- Children can make all of the sounds.

- Children start and stop the correct sound by following the teacher's nonverbal directions.

- The rain storm progresses with no silences between start and finish.

Follow-up

- Use instruments or other sound sources to replace body sounds.
- Have students decide on a sequence of sounds to make various types of rain storms.
- Provide opportunities for children to be the leaders.

Singing and playing instruments: Children experiment with a variety of instruments and other sound sources.

Objective

- Children and parents will interact to explore and create sound sources from materials found at home.

Materials

- A letter to the parents describing the activity and asking for help in assembling the instruments

- Instruments or pictures of instruments from various cultures that are made from natural or found materials (for example, shakers or drums made from gourds, steel drums, log drums, spoons)

- Song to accompany, such as "Band of Angels" in *150 American Folk Songs* edited by Peter Erdei (New York: Boosey & Hawkes, 1974)

Prior Knowledge and Experiences

- Children have played classroom instruments and experimented with various sound sources.

- Children know the song selected to accompany.

Procedures

1. Discuss how people around the world have made drums and shakers as well as other instruments from objects in their environment. Show actual instruments or pictures and discuss what they are made from.

2. Take from a bag, one at a time, an assortment of different containers that came from home. These may include a large can, oatmeal box, empty plastic bottles or containers with lids, paper plates, paper towel roll. Also present some dry ingredients, such as rice, and some "membranes," such as plastic wrap or wax paper.

3. Ask questions to engage children how best to put these materials together to make a drum or shaker. Call on children to experiment with different combinations that make different sounds and to describe the differences ("one is louder," "one sounds higher").

4. Give an assignment to make a drum or a shaker at home. Send home a letter explaining the project that sets a due date, or a letter that asks children to bring containers and other materials to school by a certain date, when the project will be completed with the assistance of parent or grandparent volunteers.

5. When the instruments are all assembled, have the children play the instruments for their classmates. See if the children can figure out what is inside the shakers, as well as identify the components of the various instruments.

6. Use the instruments (only a few at a time so their unique sounds can be heard) to accompany a song, such as the refrain of "Band of Angels."

Indicators of Success

- Children use a variety of sound sources to create their instruments.
- Children show their instruments with pride and enjoy playing them.

Follow-up

- Continue to collect and create different types of objects that can be turned into instruments and experiment with the varied sound possibilities.

Singing and playing instruments: Children play simple melodies and accompaniments on instruments.

Objective

- Children will strum steady beats on an Autoharp/ChromAharp, maintaining their own tempo.

Materials

- "Do, Do, Pity My Case" in *150 American Folk Songs* edited by Peter Erdei (New York: Boosey & Hawkes, 1974) and *American Folksongs for Children* by Ruth Crawford Seeger (Garden City, NY: Doubleday, 1980)
- Chorded zither (such as Autoharp or ChromAharp)

Prior Knowledge and Experiences

- Children have experience keeping a beat on simple percussion instruments while the teacher follows their tempo to sing a song.
- Children have sung the song and improvised new verses to it.

Procedures

1. Sing "Do, Do, Pity My Case" using the words "my floor to sweep when I get home" for the phrase denoting the actions. While singing, use one hand as the "bristles" of a broom, "sweeping" down the opposite leg repeatedly from the top of the leg to the knee (approximating strumming) with a strong rhythmic pulse. Ask children to join in.

2. Sing the song for the children while accompanying with an Autoharp/ChromAharp. Invite the children to perform the "sweeping" motion on the beat.

3. Tell the children that there is a special word for the "sweeping" motion when we use it to make music by playing on the strings of Autoharps/ChromAharps or guitars: "strumming."

4. Place the instrument on the floor in front of a child; ask the child to strum across the strings. Press the chord buttons for the appropriate changes, and sing the song to the tempo of the child's strumming.

5. Allow each child to have a turn as long as the group maintains attention. Keep a list of who has had a turn, and provide turns to the rest of the children later in the day or at another time.

Indicators of Success

- Children strum the strings with a steady beat, maintaining their own tempo.

Follow-up

- Children may strum other songs while the teacher fingers the chords.
- Demonstrate how two children can play together a familiar one-chord song such as "Are You Sleeping?"—with one child holding down a chord button while a second child strums. Have an Autoharp/ChromAharp available for this activity during free play time.
- Using a guitar, children can strum while the teacher fingers the chords.

Singing and playing instruments: Children play simple melodies and accompaniments on instruments.

Objective

- Children will perform simple rhythmic ostinatos (short, repeated patterns) to accompany a rhyme.

Materials

- Nursery rhyme or song with a galloping rhythm, such as "The Farmer in the Dell" in *150 American Folk Songs* edited by Peter Erdei (New York: Boosey & Hawkes, 1974) and "Ride a Cock-Horse to Banbury Cross" in *Music for Little People* by John Feierabend (New York: Boosey & Hawkes, 1986); or with a trotting rhythm, such as "Riding in a Buggy" in *The Melody Book,* 2d ed., by Patricia Hackett (Englewood Cliffs, NJ: Prentice-Hall, 1992), and "Bell Horses" in *Share the Music,* Grade K (New York: Macmillan/ McGraw-Hill, 1995)

- Six or eight paper or plastic cups (or half coconut shells)

Prior Knowledge and Experiences

- Children are familiar with the rhyme.

Procedures

1. Recite the rhyme to be sure all children are very familiar with it.

2. Have children pat their legs to make a "galloping" pattern (use alternate hands on legs to create a long/short/long/short/long ostinato pattern). Speak the rhyme to this rhythmic accompaniment. Repeat several times until the children are comfortable (if this pattern is too difficult for the children, modify rhythm to a simple steady beat representing "trotting").

3. Bring out two paper or plastic cups (or shells). Use the cups upside down on the floor to play the pattern (to sound like the horses' hooves). Pass out several pairs of cups for children to play while everyone else recites the rhyme. Repeat so that all children have a turn.

Indicators of Success

- Children maintain the rhythmic ostinato while they and/or their classmates chant a rhyme.

Follow-up

- Add jingle bells, or wrist or ankle bells, playing them on the steady beat.

- Replace paper cups with wooden percussion instruments (this will increase the difficulty of the activity considerably, because while the alternating physical motion used to play the cups sets up the rhythm pattern in a very natural manner, many of the children may not yet have developed the muscle control and rhythmic sense required to play the repeated pattern on sticks or woodblocks).

Singing and playing instruments: Children play simple melodies and accompaniments on instruments.

Objective

- Children will figure out how to play simple melodies or patterns from melodies by ear.

Materials

- Three resonator bells (G, A, B) placed in order in a box top or on a mat with the bell outlines drawn, so the children will be able to place them in sequence easily by matching the bell with its outline—a xylophone with all but those three bars removed would also work

Prior Knowledge and Experiences

- Children know the song "Old MacDonald."
- Children have had exploratory experiences with resonator bells.

Procedures

1. Introduce activity in large or small groups, for children to do during free play or center/small-group time.

2. Sing the "ee-i-ee-i-o" part of "Old MacDonald" several times to be sure the children know it well (it is important to use G as the starting pitch for this pattern). Tell them that the three bells in the music center can sing that part of the song, too. The children's job is to figure out how to play them so they sound like "ee-i-ee-i-o." Show them how to place the bells on their outlines, like a puzzle, to be sure that the bells are in order.

3. During free play or center/small-group time, children will experiment with the bells to find the pattern.

4. Once all children have had several turns to learn the pattern (during the course of several days if necessary), sing the song as a group while children take turns playing. Be sure to use G as the starting pitch for the song to correspond with the bells when they enter.

Indicators of Success

- Children figure out the correct pattern on the bells and play it at the appropriate place in the song.

Follow-up

- Ask the children to figure out how many of the bells are needed to play the phrase "here a chick, there a chick, everywhere a chick, chick." When they have concluded that just one is needed, have them use the G bell to accompany that part of the song.

- Introduce other simple, familiar songs the children can learn through experimentation, such as "Hot Cross Buns" or "Mary Had a Little Lamb."

Singing and playing instruments: Children play simple melodies and accompaniments on instruments.

Objective

- Children will perform a simple melodic ostinato (short, repeated pattern of pitches) to accompany singing.

Materials

- "See-Saw, Margery Daw" or "See Saw Up and Down" in *The Kodály Method,* 2d ed., by Lois Choksy (Englewood Cliffs, NJ: Prentice-Hall, 1988)
- Two resonator bells, Cs or Ds pitched one octave (eight notes) apart, and/or xylophone or metallophone with bars removed to isolate the octave pitches (either Cs or Ds)

Prior Knowledge and Experiences

- Children know the song.
- Children have had exploratory experiences with the instruments used.

Procedures

1. Have the children sit crosslegged on the floor with their hands out to their sides, palms flat on the floor. With a steady beat, rock back and forth by shifting weight from hand to hand. Sing the song accompanied by the rocking.

2. Demonstrate how the back-and-forth, "see-saw" motion can be transferred to the instrument, playing with a steady beat the pattern "low, high, low, high" to accompany the song.

3. Provide turns for children to play the instrument. Help them establish the steady "see-saw" motion on the instrument, and then bring in the singers (if using C bells, start song on the pitch G; if using D bells, start song on the pitch A).

Indicators of Success

- Children play the alternating pitch pattern with a steady beat to accompany the singing. (If this is too difficult for some children, they may play the two pitches simultaneously rather than alternately.)

Follow-up

- Use a similar pattern of two pitches, either an octave or fifth (C and G, or D and A), to accompany familiar one-chord or pentatonic songs such as "Row, Row, Row Your Boat" or "Are You Sleeping?"

Singing and playing instruments: Children play simple melodies and accompaniments on instruments.

Objective

- Children will play pitches of an ascending or descending scale to accompany melody scale songs, with teacher cues or independently.

Materials

- Songs with melodies that move consecutively up or down the diatonic scale, such as "The Snowman" in *Music: A Way of Life for the Young Child* by Kathleen Bayless and Marjorie Ramsey (Columbus, OH: Merrill, 1987); "Hot Dog" and "Pussy Willow" in *Musical Games, Finger Plays, and Rhythmic Activities for Early Childhood* by Marian Wirth, Verna Stassevitch, Rita Shotwell, and Patricia Stemmler (West Nyack, NY: Parker, 1983); "Freddy Flea," "One Potato, Two Potato," or teacher-created lyrics

- Resonator bells on steps, step bells, or bell lyre placed upright ladder-style so low bars are at the bottom

- Prop or visual aid related to the song

Prior Knowledge and Experiences

- Children have had experience playing resonator bells.

Procedures

1. Provide a visual focus, either a small prop or an illustration of something related to the song. Introduce the song to a small group of children. Tell them that the song will have some musical sounds that go up and down to tell a story. Sing the song while gradually moving the prop higher and lower with the changes in pitch.

2. Ask the children to move their arms up and down like the prop while you sing. Repeat, moving the whole body up and down.

3. Bring out the bells. While singing, move the prop up and down the bells, to correspond to the pitch changes. Demonstrate how the bells can be played (the mallet moves up and down as the prop did).

4. Invite children, one at a time, to play the song. Using the prop, help them to know when to move to the next bell. Follow the child's tempo when needed to ensure success. Gradually withdraw the prop as he or she becomes independent in hearing when the pitches change. It is not important that the child play the exact rhythm, since the pitch changes are the focus of the activity.

Indicators of Success

- Children play simple scale-wise songs on the bells, following teacher cues or independently.

Follow-up

- Place bells in music corner so children may use them for independent play and experimentation.

- Teach additional songs with scale passages that the children can play.

- Encourage children to create their own up-and-down songs.

Creating music: Children improvise songs to
accompany their play activities.

Objective

- Children will express their
  ideas in spontaneous singing.

Materials

- Two small wooden figures or
  wooden-spoon puppets

Prior Knowledge and Experiences

- The teacher has demonstrated
  spontaneous singing by giving
  instructions and telling stories
  using a singing voice.

Procedures

1. Using two small wooden figures as puppets, demonstrate a dialogue between them using improvised singing.

2. Invite individual children to take turns holding one of the figures and participating in a singing discussion with the other figure, which you are holding. Replace the teacher/child pair with child/child pairs when children are comfortable with the activity.

3. Place the figures in a music center or play area to encourage additional spontaneous singing during playtime.

Indicators of Success

- Children create spontaneous songs while playing with the figures, with other dolls or puppets, or without the assistance of props.

Follow-up

- Provide a variety of pictures or scenes to use as backdrops for the figures to stimulate more elaborate improvisations.

Creating music: Children improvise songs to accompany their play activities.

Objective

- Children will create singing telephone conversations.

Materials

- Pretend "telephones" (for example, three pieces of curved PVC piping, 2″ in diameter, hooked together to form a "C")

Prior Knowledge and Experiences

- Children have experienced singing both in a group and by themselves.

Procedures

1. Introduce the new "telephones" by showing one to a group of children. Ask the children what this thing could be. Encourage discussion and manipulation of the object.

2. Tell children that this is a special "singing telephone." Whenever it is used, everyone is encouraged to sing rather than talk. Demonstrate by singing "hello" into one end. Hold the instrument up to a child, and encourage that child to respond by singing "hello," as well. Continue modeling by singing a question into the instrument such as "What's your favorite book, Taylor?" Children will then be encouraged to sing about a book or story.

3. Place several "singing telephones" in the music center for the children's use. Children can sing about their favorite books, animals, or anything else they choose.

4. During free play, interact with children who need some encouragement. Model singing conversations in a variety of pitches, tempos, and rhythm patterns, thus encouraging children to be more exploratory.

Indicators of Success

- Children become more and more comfortable singing freely.
- Children initiate their own singing conversations with other children, a teacher, or by themselves.

Follow-up

- Use singing conversations whenever opportunities arise in the course of daily classroom activities.

Creating music: Children improvise songs to
accompany their play activities.

Objective

- Children will identify the functional use of music to assist ordinary work activities and will create songs to accompany their own daily activities.

Materials

- "Grinding Corn" in *The Music Connection,* Grade 1 (Morristown, NJ: Silver Burdett Ginn, 1995)

- "Looby Loo" in *Shake It to the One That You Love Best* by Cheryl Warren Mattox (El Sabrante, CA: Warren-Mattox Productions, 1989)

- *Corn Is Maize* by Aliki (New York: Crowell Press, 1976)

Prior Knowledge and Experiences

- Children have experience dramatizing or pantomiming song lyrics.

Procedures

1. Sing the song "Grinding Corn." Discuss the importance of corn to the Native Americans, what the ground corn (meal) would be used for, and why someone might sing while grinding. Read and discuss the book *Corn Is Maize* (or use as a resource).

2. Sing the refrain of "Looby Loo." Explain that this song is about taking a bath a long time ago, in the days when it was difficult because the water had to be heated and carried to a big wooden tub. People only took baths once a week or on special occasions. With the children, discover how putting one hand or foot in, as the game is played, came from testing to see how hot the water was, and that "shake, shake, shake" is shaking dry.

3. Play the complete game. Discuss why people might sing a song to make the bath more enjoyable (maybe they know someone who sings in the shower at home!).

4. Discuss both songs with relation to how music is often used to make work or daily activities easier or more enjoyable.

5. Have the children choose some ordinary work activities to pantomime or dramatize (for example, setting the table, bathing the baby, ironing the laundry). Ask for volunteers to make up a song to accompany the activity.

6. Encourage the children to create songs throughout the day to accompany their activities.

Indicators of Success

- Children spontaneously create songs to accompany their daily activities.

- Children explain the functional use of music in work and daily life.

Follow-up

- Continue to add songs about work and daily activities to the children's repertoire (for example, "Here We Go 'Round the Mulberry Bush," "Cobbler Mend My Shoe," "I've Been Working on the Railroad").

Creating music: Children improvise songs to accompany their play activities.

Objective

- Children improvise short songs as they are sung by characters in a picture book.

Materials

- Picture book in which a character sings; for example, *Lizard's Song* by George Shannon, Jose Aruego, and Ariene Dewey (New York: Greenwillow, 1981) or *Tacky the Penguin* by Helen Lester (Boston: Houghton Mifflin, 1988)

Prior Knowledge and Experiences

- Children have experience singing alone in singing games and activities.

Procedures

1. Introduce the book, explaining that one of the characters will be singing a song throughout the story. As you read the book to them, ask the children to notice every time the character sings. (If the words to the character's song are provided, chant them rhythmically each time so the children will learn them.)

2. Ask children to volunteer to make up and sing a short song that they think the character might be singing. If the words were provided, children may choose to use them, or to create their own, or to use a neutral syllable such as "la." Encourage children to create a song that does not sound like anyone else's song.

3. Read the book again, asking a different child to sing the character's song each time the character sings it in the story.

Indicators of Success

- Children improvise short songs that do not directly imitate other children's songs.

Follow-up

- Place the book in a reading corner or music corner so children can return to the activity independently.

- Repeat the activity with a different story, create an original class story that includes singing characters, or have the children find places to add songs to stories that don't explicitly mention them.

Creating music: Children improvise songs to accompany their play activities.

Objective

- Children sing dialogue while acting out a story to create an "opera."

Materials

- Selected story or fairy tale (shorter stories are best in the beginning)
- Props appropriate for selected story

Prior Knowledge and Experiences

- Children know the story line well.
- Children know the difference between their singing voice and their speaking voice.
- Children have experience singing improvised questions and answers and dialogues similar to those in the other teaching examples provided for this standard.

Procedures

1. Review a familiar and favorite story (for example, "The Three Bears").

2. Assign various roles to children who volunteer to participate in singing the story.

3. Narrate the story in a general way while children act out the scene using singing voices in dialogue. Example: You say, "Bears are in the kitchen. Mama is making porridge. Sing what they may be saying." Mama Bear sings, "This is too hot for us to eat." Daddy Bear sings, "Then let's go for a walk in the woods." Baby Bear sings, "Can I go, too?" Daddy Bear sings "Yes, let's go." Dialogue should be created by children rather than memorized.

4. At various places in this children's opera, you may find places to have all the children sing a familiar song as a chorus (for example, when Goldilocks falls asleep in the bed, all children could sing a lullaby.) Some children may also volunteer to sing a short solo, as an aria.

Indicators of Success

- Children use their singing instead of speaking voices.
- Children react to one another in dialogue appropriate to the story line.
- Children volunteer to be chorus members or soloists..

Follow-up

- Use a new story to create another opera.
- Add sound effects made by children at appropriate times in the story.
- Perform opera with costumes and props for parents or other children.
- Attend an opera for children or view one on videotape (for example, *Hansel and Gretel*).

STANDARD 2B

Creating music: Children improvise instrumental accompaniments to songs, recorded selections, stories, and poems.

Objective

- Children will choose sounds from nontraditional sound sources ("found instruments") thoughtfully to accompany familiar songs.

Materials

- Any objects normally available in the classroom and kitchen

Prior Knowledge and Experiences

- Children have a repertoire of songs they know well.

Procedures

1. Have the children search the classroom/kitchen area for "found instruments," things that make interesting sounds either alone or together. Explore the sounds made by everyday objects, such as blocks, Legos, or bristle blocks scraped with different objects; graters; spoons; different sizes of tubs; different substances in tubs such as oatmeal, popcorn, sand, jingle bells, and marbles.

2. Have the children bring their found instruments and sit in a circle (the circle will allow them to see the other instruments). Have each child demonstrate his or her instrument. Lead a group discussion on what the sounds remind the children of or make them think about.

3. Have the children think of familiar songs that match the sounds, or name songs and have the children choose the found instruments that best match them. Encourage the children to explain their decisions. For example, children may decide the scraping sounds remind them of the "quack, quack, quack" part in "Six Little Ducks," or the shakers may remind them of "Shake My Sillies Out."

4. Sing the songs suggested, with several children accompanying on the found instruments that the group deemed most appropriate. Make sure all children have a turn by suggesting or hinting at additional songs if necessary. (Explain that everyone will have a turn, but only a few for each song, because when everyone plays at the same time it is too noisy to hear the special sound of each instrument.)

Indicators of Success

- Children create found instruments using a variety of interesting objects or combinations of objects.

- Children choose sounds to accompany songs thoughtfully, by relating the sounds to words or ideas expressed in familiar sounds.

- Children experiment with found-instrument sounds during free choice time.

Follow-up

- Use traditional classroom instruments to experiment with creating accompaniments that are appropriate for familiar songs.

- Try several different instruments or combinations to accompany the same song, and discuss which sounded best and why.

Creating music: Children improvise instrumental accompaniments
to songs, recorded selections, stories, and poems.

Objective

- Children create or choose
  sounds and movements to
  improvise sound effects and
  motions as an accompaniment
  for a song and a recorded
  selection.

Materials

- "Little Red Caboose" in
  *Musical Games, Fingerplays,
  and Rhythmic Activities for
  Early Childhood* by Marian
  Wirth, Verna Stassevitch, Rita
  Shotwell, and Patricia
  Stemmler (West Nyack, NY:
  Parker, 1983) and *The Music
  Connection,* Grade K (Morris-
  town, NJ: Silver Burdett
  Ginn, 1995); or "Down by
  the Station" in *The Melody
  Book,* 2d ed., by Patricia
  Hackett (Englewood Cliffs,
  NJ: Prentice-Hall, 1992)

- "The Little Train of Caipira"
  from *Bachianas Brasileiras* by
  Hector Villa-Lobos (recording)

- Audio-playback equipment

- A variety of sound sources

Prior Knowledge and Experiences

- Children have learned to sing
  the song selected.

- If possible, children have
  watched and listened to a
  train.

Procedures

1. Sing the song together to review.

2. Draw responses from the children about what sounds would be
   heard while riding in a train, while waiting at the station, while
   working on the tracks, and so forth.

3. Decide on ways to produce the sounds suggested, using any sound
   sources available (for example, a woodblock for a hammering
   sound, sandpaper blocks and maracas for the train wheels, voices or
   a whistle for the train whistle, voices for the engineer).

4. Choose places in the song to add the sounds and assign a few children to each sound (remind them that the song will be repeated
   until everyone has had a turn).

5. Have children create an introduction to the song by improvising
   with the various sounds until teacher gives a stop signal. Sing the
   song with the accompanying sounds. Add an ending with the
   sounds again, fading them away to silence.

6. Play the recording of "The Little Train of Caipira," asking children
   to listen to the ways a composer created music about a train.
   Discuss what they heard.

7. Have children demonstrate motions that might be used by the people working on the railroad or on the train, the motion of the
   wheels, and so on. Play the piece for the children to accompany
   with improvised motions.

8. If the children are still interested, or on another day, assign children various train sounds to use to create an improvisation to
   accompany the piece. Discuss the necessity to perform quietly so
   they can still hear the music. Children who are waiting for a turn
   may accompany the music with the motions.

Indicators of Success

- Children make or choose sounds and motions associated with rail-
  roads or trains and use them to accompany the song and recording.

Follow-up

- Introduce other songs and stories about trains (for example, "Engine, Engine, Number Nine," "Orange Blossom Special," "The Little Engine That Could").

- Use a similar activity to create accompaniments for other children's songs or musical selections with different sounds that may be imitated (for example, music about boats and the sea).

Creating music: Children improvise instrumental accompaniments to songs, recorded selections, stories, and poems.

Objective

- Children will use classroom instruments to simulate environmental sounds, creating sound effects to enhance songs.

Materials

- "Old House" in *The Music Connection,* Grade 1 (Morristown, NJ: Silver Burdett Ginn, 1995)
- Assorted classroom instruments

Prior Knowledge and Experiences

- Children have created sound effects for songs and stories.
- If possible, children have watched some work on a house being constructed.

Procedures

1. Have the children name some things in and around the classroom that are made of wood (bookshelves, door, window frames, tables). Introduce the idea that a person who builds or repairs things made of wood is a carpenter.

2. Ask the children to listen for the tools that the carpenter needs to build a new house. Sing the second verse of "Old House" (about building) and have the children answer (hammer and saw).

3. Demonstrate some instruments and have children decide if they sound like hammering or sawing (for example, hammering might be represented by a palm-held cowbell struck with mallet, sawing might be represented by a scraped guiro or notched sticks). Sounds representing sanding the wood (sandblocks) and painting (rubbing hand on drumhead) may be added.

4. Have the children decide where to add these sounds, and sing and play the verse accordingly. Children without instruments may pantomime the activity.

5. Sing the first verse (tearing the house down) for the children. Ask them to discuss ways to tear down the house and the sounds that would result. Experiment with instruments to represent these sounds (for example, wind chimes for breaking glass, big drum for wrecking ball, cymbals played with a felt mallet for the collapsing building). Have the children help add these sounds to the song.

6. Have the children create an introduction and/or conclusion to the song, using their sounds.

7. Perform the complete piece, providing opportunities for trading instruments as necessary.

Indicators of Success

- Children choose instrumental sounds to create appropriate sounds and atmosphere for the song.

Follow-up

- Use instruments to provide sounds or set the mood to accompany other songs or poems where sounds are implied by the text (for example, "Hickory Dickory Dock").

Creating music: Children improvise instrumental accompaniments to songs, recorded selections, stories, and poems.

Objective

- Children will accompany a familiar story with improvisation on classroom instruments.

Materials

- Assorted classroom instruments
- Familiar children's story or fairy tale, for example, "Three Billy Goats Gruff," "Goldilocks and the Three Bears," or "Chicken Little"
- Cut-out pictures of the main characters in the story and of the instruments that may be used in the accompaniment
- Feltboard, chalkboard tray, or easel

Prior Knowledge and Experiences

- The story has been read to the children on several occasions.

Procedures

1. Show the cover of the book and ask the children to tell you the story. As they mention each main character, place the picture of that character on a feltboard, chalkboard tray, or easel.

2. Explain that today, when you tell the story, they will accompany it by playing instruments to represent the main characters. Each time you say the name of the character, that instrument will play. For instance, they may want a drum to represent the Troll in "Three Billy Goats Gruff," so every time his name is spoken, the children with the drums will play a short improvisation. Explain that they may play as long as you point to the picture of the character.

3. As the children decide which instruments will represent which character, place a picture of that instrument below or next to the character's picture to serve as a reminder. Distribute instruments.

4. Tell the story, directing the instrumentation by pointing to the characters to cue the improvisations.

5. If there are not enough instruments for all children to participate initially, stop partway through the story to give turns, or repeat the activity.

Indicators of Success

- Children play at the appropriate times.
- Children enjoy the activity and reproduce it during free-play time.

Follow-up

- Use different stories as stimuli for improvisation.

Creating music: Children improvise instrumental accompaniments to songs, recorded selections, stories, and poems.

Objective

- Children will improvise "songs" on pitched percussion instruments during dramatic play.

Materials

- "Rabbit and the Hyena Play the Sanza" by Ann Pellowski in *The Story Vine* (New York: Macmillan, 1984)
- Xylophone or other pitched percussion instrument such as melody bells

Prior Knowledge and Experiences

- Children know the story well.
- Children have had exploratory experiences with the instrument and know the proper way it should be played.

Procedures

1. Review the story, with the children supplying as much of the story line as possible.

2. Explain that one of the activity corners or centers for free play time will be the "Rabbit and Hyena" corner. Children may go there two at a time to play-act based on the story, making up their own musical composition on the instrument (other children may watch if they choose). Monitor the time children spend with the activity so that some children do not monopolize it, perhaps by setting a simple kitchen timer to designate the length of turns.

Indicators of Success

- Children incorporate instrumental improvisation during dramatic play based on the story.

Follow-up

- Provide the same or different instruments in a play corner or center and encourage the children to create their own story or dramatic play using the instrument.

Creating music: Children create short pieces of music, using voices, instruments, and other sound sources.

Objective

- Children will compose sound patterns to represent different characters in a story.

Materials

- *Silly Sally* by Audrey Wood (San Diego: Harcourt Brace Jovanovich, 1993) or any other story in which characters are added one at a time (for example, "Henny Penny")
- Assorted classroom percussion instruments

Prior Knowledge and Experiences

- Children have had exploratory experiences with the classroom instruments.
- Children have experience clapping and playing short rhythm patterns.
- Children know the story *Silly Sally.*

Procedures

1. Have children echo the pattern below with clapping and chanting a few times until they can perform it independently.

$$\frac{4}{4} \quad | \quad | \quad | \quad | \quad \sqcap \quad \sqcap \quad | \quad |$$

Sil - ly Sal - ly Sil-ly Sil-ly Sal-ly

2. Read the story. Every time Silly Sally's name is read, clap and chant the rhythm pattern.

3. Look through the book to identify the characters. Choose an instrument for each character and distribute instruments to the children.

4. Practice playing the pattern on the instruments. Children without instruments can play along on their legs, or tap their forefingers together, or pat their heads. Chanting the words quietly will help them play the rhythm.

5. Read the book, asking children to play the pattern every time their instrument's character appears. When more then one is mentioned, the pattern is played by each instrument in the same order as the characters. Because a character is added to the story each time Silly Sally sets off for town, the composition will get longer and longer.

6. Repeat to provide turns for every child if necessary.

Indicators of Success

- Children play the patterns for the correct character and create an additive piece of music.

Follow-up

- Tape-record the activity and make the tape and book available for individual listening.
- Once children are very familiar with the story and associated sounds, have them tape-record the story, cueing them to play the instrument instead of identifying the character. Listen to the recording and have children identify each character as it appears.
- Create a different word/rhythm pattern for each character.
- Instead of using rhythm patterns, help the children create and practice a short, easy melodic theme for each character.

Creating music: Children create short pieces of music, using voices, instruments, and other sound sources.

Objective

- Children will use and respond to gestures indicating duration to create short sound pieces.

Materials

- Classroom instruments or other sound sources

Prior Knowledge and Experiences

- Children have experience giving attention to a leader, transferring attention from one leader to another, and being a leader.
- Children have experience playing classroom instruments.

Procedures

1. With a small group of children, demonstrate one gesture for "play" and one for "stop." For example, use open hands for play and closed fists for stop, or use the American Sign Language gestures.

2. Give children instruments and ask them to play their instruments when you show the gesture for play and to stop playing when you show the gesture for stop. Let this be a game, giving verbal and visual reinforcement when they are successful at following the conducting gestures.

3. Explain that the leader of a musical group is called a "conductor."

4. Encourage students to take turns being the conductor; participate by playing a child's instrument while the child conducts the group. Provide turns for all children who volunteer.

Indicators of Success

- Children follow the leader's gestures successfully.
- Children choose to lead a group sound piece.
- Children initiate the activity during free choice time.

Follow-up

- Have children help create gestures representing contrasting musical ideas such as loud and soft, fast and slow, and so forth.
- Have the children with same or similar instruments sit in groups, and have the conductor decide which group(s) should play. Children can decide how the conductor will indicate when each group should start and stop.
- Attend the rehearsal of a musical ensemble to watch how the conductor leads the group using gestures, or view a conductor on videotape (for example, Walt Disney's *Fantasia*).

Creating music: Children create short pieces of music, using voices, instruments, and other sound sources.

Objective

- Children will use classroom instruments to create "sound interpretations" of songs or poems.

Materials

- "Twinkle, Twinkle, Little Star"
- Assorted classroom instruments

Prior Knowledge and Experiences

- Children are familiar with the song.
- Children have experience with classroom instruments.

Procedures

1. Sing the song together as a review.

2. Have children imagine what it would sound like if they could hear stars twinkle, and brainstorm for descriptive words (high, far away, quiet, tinkling, sparkling).

3. Ask children which instruments would make sounds most like those they described. Bring out instruments they suggest and experiment; let the children to decide if they are suitable. Instruments that they forget about may also be brought out for them to try. (Try not to impose adult ideas of appropriateness, but be sure the children have reasons for their decisions.)

4. Pass out four or five instruments at a time for children to play to accompany the song. Repeat until all children have had a turn.

5. Ask the children to decide on two or three instruments to play only during the "twinkle" phrases and two or three to play only in the middle section. Once the children can play at the appropriate time, see if they can play while only whispering the song, then only mouthing the song to help them keep their places while playing.

Indicators of Success

- Children make choices of instruments to accompany the song that relate to the song in a way that they can explain.

Follow-up

- Repeat the activity with different songs.
- Create a longer composition by adding an introduction, coda, and/or interludes between repetitions of the song.

Creating music: Children create short pieces of music, using voices, instruments, and other sound sources.

Objective

- Children will compose a song to sing while telling a story.

Materials

- "Gunniwolf" from *The People Could Fly* edited by Virginia Hamilton (New York: Alfred A. Knopf, 1985)
- Resonator bells, xylophone, or small electronic keyboard

Prior Knowledge and Experiences

- Children have had experience playing and improvising on the instruments used.

Procedures

1. Tell the story of "Gunniwolf," emphasizing the important role the song plays in the story.

2. Ask the children to help create a song for the little girl to sing (working with small groups of children, instead of the whole group, will allow for more participation and facilitate this activity). Use children's ideas for words to create one or two very short phrases. Provide children with five resonator bells, or remove all but five bars from a xylophone, to create a pentatonic scale (pitches C, D, E, G, A work well; on a keyboard, use the first 5 black notes above middle C). Have the children use the instrument to experiment with matching notes to words to find a pattern they think makes a good song. When they have a pattern they like, help them repeat it, and write it down for future reference. Sing it several times until the children know it well.

3. Still in the small group, tell the story, with the children singing the song every time it occurs (children engaged in free play or other activities may be invited to come listen as well).

4. Repeat the activity so all children have a chance to participate.

5. During large-group time, tell the story again, asking for a different group to sing its song each time the girl sings in the story. It may be helpful to sing or play the song once for the children before they sing if they have trouble remembering it.

Indicators of Success

- Children create the text and melody of a simple song and sing it during the telling of the story.

Follow-up

- Make the instruments available for the children to use to create songs individually.
- Encourage children to create songs to use in other stories, plays, or activities (for example, children could create a "going-out-to-play" song).

Creating music: Children create short pieces of music, using voices, instruments, and other sound sources.

Objective

- Children will create a piece of music using vocal and mouth sounds to interpret peers' gestures.

Materials

- None required

Prior Knowledge and Experiences

- Children have had exploratory experiences with sounds that can be made with the mouth and with the voice.

Procedures

1. Have each child make a favorite sound with his or her voice or mouth. Make sure through prior experiences that children are aware of a variety of options.

2. One at a time, have each child make a sound while the other children make a gesture with their hands or body that "shows" the sound. Explore a variety of physical gestures that might represent the sound, and explore a wide variety of sounds that might represent each gesture.

3. Have a child be the "conductor." Have the child do a repetitive motion and have the "ensemble" interpret the motion through their sounds. Just as all instruments in a band do not sound alike, all children do not have to make the same sound to represent the motion.

4. Once children are comfortable with the activity, the teacher may cue the conducting child when to change to a new motion, which would in turn cue different sounds from the group. It is important that the conductor make one motion repetitively prior to switching to a new motion, since random movements are hard to interpret vocally because there is little response time.

5. Record the sound pieces created. Play them a few times and let the children experiment with different movements to interpret the sounds (they need not move in the same way as the leader did). Make the recordings available for children to use during free play time.

Indicators of Success

- Children are creative in using new body motions and unusual sound interpretations.
- Children volunteer to be the leader.
- Sound interpretations have at least some of the characteristics of the motions.

Follow-up

- Use other sound sources besides mouth and voice.
- Videotape a performance and let children watch and listen to their creations.

Creating music: Children invent and use original graphic or symbolic systems to represent vocal and instrumental sounds and musical ideas.

Objective

- Children will experiment with sounds, design an icon for one sound, and create pieces of music by sequencing icons for performance.

Materials

- White construction paper, black crayons or markers
- Sound sources

Prior Knowledge and Experiences

- Children should have the pre-reading skill of scanning a sequence of pictures or written material from left to right.

Procedures

1. Individually, help each child choose a unique sound using the voice, body, or other sound source and devise and draw an icon to represent the sound.

2. In small or large groups, ask children to show their icons individually and make their sound. Have the other children imitate the sound while the child holds the icon. Each child should have access to each sound source.

3. One "composer" chooses two sounds from those heard. The two children stand next to one another holding up their icons in the order determined by the composer.

4. The composer points to the first one, and all the children begin making the sound and repeating it, until the composer decides it is time for a new sound and points to the second icon. The composer may switch between sounds as he or she chooses. (The teacher may need to give a cue to end the composition.)

5. Expand the number of icons used to create a more complex sequence of sounds.

6. When the activity is familiar, use the icons leaning against blackboard, rather than held by children, so the class "reads" the composition rather than associates the sound with an individual child.

Indicators of Success

- Children can identify a unique sound source readily available to them.

- Children create a visual image to represent a sound. Children remember each unique sound represented by individual icons.

- Children have specific ideas for selecting and sequencing sounds.

Follow-up

- Use a blank sheet for rests among the sound sources.

- Choose sound sources that can be produced loudly and softly. Put the same icon on two different colors of paper (for example, pink = soft, red = loud). Children perform sounds with dynamic contrasts.

- Assign only certain children to "play" each icon, as if they were playing in a band.

Creating music: Children invent and use original graphic or symbolic systems to represent vocal and instrumental sounds and musical ideas.

Objective

- Children respond to iconic (line) representations of pitch and will create their own music maps and perform them with their voices.

Materials

- Large blank pieces of paper
- Thick-line markers
- A puppet with a mouth that moves
- A large piece of paper with original line notation similar to the model below:

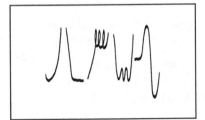

Prior Knowledge and Experiences

- Experience with different vocal pitch levels (see page 17).

Procedures

1. Ask children to echo the puppet. "Puppet" uses the syllable "oo," gliding from pitch to pitch without separation, starting with short up-and-down patterns, then increasing in length and complexity.

2. Tell the children that you have a new kind of song that you can't figure out how to sing. Ask the children and the puppet to help you learn how to sing the song. Show the class a large piece of paper with iconic pitch notation (a music map—see example at left).

3. Encourage children to follow the direction and shapes of the lines with their voices, again singing on the "oo." (The puppet may assist by following along the lines with a stick to keep everyone together.) Perform the piece and discuss how it could be performed a different way. Experiment with other vocal sounds or words the children suggest.

4. Create a melody as a class using line notation. Have children offer ideas for interesting lines and shapes to follow. Experiment on a chalkboard or scratch paper before transferring them to the music map.

5. Distribute paper and markers. Have the children create their own pieces and draw them using line notation. Children may perform their pieces alone and/or lead other children to follow their map. Display the maps in the classroom.

Indicators of Success

- Children participate in the decoding and creation of iconic (line) notation representing pitch.

Follow-up

- Find objects in the room or playground with interesting shapes (for example, toy train tracks, a slide, an easel). Have the children "sing" the shapes by following with their voices as you or a child outline the shape of the object with a hand or pointer.

- Present two maps to the children, perform one of them several times, and have the children figure out and explain which you performed.

Creating music: Children invent and use original graphic or symbolic systems to represent vocal and instrumental sounds and musical ideas.

Objective

- Students will create representations of contrasting pieces of music using movement and symbols.

Materials

- "Ballet of the Unhatched Chicks" from *Pictures at an Exhibition* by Modeste Mussorgsky and "Air on a G String" by J. S. Bach (or other recordings of two contrasting pieces)
- Audio-playback equipment
- Crayons or markers and paper

Prior Knowledge and Experiences

- Children have listened to and moved to music in various styles and tempos.

Procedures

1. Initiate the following fingerplay using slow, "smooth" speech for lines one and two and fast, detached speech for lines three and four. (Hand is the snail, arm is the rail; hand is the mouse, body is the house):

   Slowly, slowly, very slowly crawls the little snail,

   Slowly, slowly, very slowly up the garden rail.

   Quickly, quickly, very quickly runs the little mouse,

   Quickly, quickly, very quickly all around the house.

2. Encourage the children to describe the differences between the two contrasting sections. Words such as slow, fast, smooth, and choppy may be used.

3. Tell the children that the music they will listen to sounds like either the snail part or mouse part of the rhyme. Encourage them to use the appropriate hand gesture from the fingerplay to show what they hear while they listen.

4. Play the beginning section of one piece and discuss it, then play the second piece, discuss it, and compare it to the first piece.

5. Give children paper and crayons and ask them to listen again and to create marks on the paper to show how the music moves (remind them to think about how their hands moved).

6. Have children show and describe their drawings. Display the papers in the classroom.

Indicators of Success

- Children respond appropriately to the musical contrasts through movement, drawing, and verbalizations.

Follow-up

- Play the musical examples for interpretation through large body movements.
- Have children "perform" their own and each other's drawings using vocal sounds.
- Repeat listening activity using different musical examples.

Creating music: Children invent and use original graphic or symbolic systems to represent vocal and instrumental sounds and musical ideas.

Objective

- Children will be able to identify themes in *Peter and the Wolf* by displaying original icons for each character.

Materials

- Sets of 4 × 6 index cards with each character's name printed at the bottom (one set of all seven character cards for each child)

- Popsicle sticks, glue, crayons (or pictures cut from magazines)

- Narrated recording of *Peter and the Wolf* by Sergey Prokofiev

- Audio-playback equipment

Prior Knowledge and Experiences

- Children have experience listening attentively to music.

- Children are familiar with *Peter and the Wolf* storyline from picture books read to them previously. Examples: *Peter and the Wolf* by Maria Carlson and Charles Mikolaycak (New York: Puffin, 1982); *Peter and the Wolf* by Josef Palecek (Natick, MA: Picture Book Studio, 1987); *Peter and the Wolf* by Michelle Lemieux (New York: Morrow Junior Books, 1991).

Procedures

1. Use the beginning of the piece, in which each character is introduced and its melody is played alone. For each character, play its melody a number of times, and have the children draw its picture on the appropriate index cards (or have pictures cut out from magazines representing each of the characters and have children glue them on cards). Glue the index cards onto popsicle sticks so the sticks become handles. Note: Make a card for one or two characters each day, until all seven have been completed. On each day, review the characters from previous days, having children hold up appropriate pictures when the narrator introduces each character. Repeat as a game until children can identify individual melodies. Adapt the activity for younger children by including fewer characters, ones that are easily recognizable and contrasting (for example, only the bird and the wolf).

2. Play the entire selection. Assign each child one character. When the child hears that character's melody, he or she should hold up the picture. This is easier in some places of the piece than in others, so you may want to have a set of pictures on the board and point to them at appropriate times.

3. Have children switch characters for subsequent listenings. Each day's listening should begin with a review of the melodies, with each child holding up each picture as a review.

Indicators of Success

- Children identify prominently played melodies in the piece by holding up their picture at the appropriate times.

- Children listen attentively to the music.

Follow-up

- When children are very familiar with the character/melody associations, each child can hold a picture for two characters: one in each hand.

- Movements for each character can be used instead of a picture, and all children could move when each melody is highlighted. (This is an easier and less time-consuming alternative for this activity.)

Creating music: Children invent and use original graphic or symbolic systems to represent vocal and instrumental sounds and musical ideas.

Objective

- Children will determine appropriate graphic symbols to represent musical events and check their "score" for accuracy.

Materials

- Recording of "From the Diary of a Fly" by Béla Bártok (arrangement by Greene String Quartet)
- Audio-playback equipment
- Large piece of paper and different colored markers

Prior Knowledge and Experiences

- Children have mirrored the teacher in performing a nonlocomotor, full-body movement sequence corresponding to aspects of the piece (pitch, articulation, texture, and so on) and have responded to questions designed to place the musical events in sequence.
- Children have experience creating original notation.

Procedures

1. Perform the movement sequence to review.

2. As you play the recording, place iconic markings on paper (in full view of children) to represent the sound at the beginning of the piece, explaining that this is your choice of a way to show the sound that corresponds to the first movement.

3. Ask children to suggest, in sequence, colors and types of symbols for remaining sections of the piece, referring as necessary back to the music and the movement sequence. Ask questions about why certain markings are appropriate, why certain colors are chosen, and other aspects. (As this is a very challenging activity, the age and experience level of the children should help determine the level of detail employed.)

4. Play the piece again, pointing to the symbols on the paper, while children perform the movements and check the accuracy of the map. Question children about any sections missing from the visual or that are inappropriately represented.

Indicators of Success

- Children choose colors and symbols appropriately to depict articulation (detached and connected), melodic direction and contour, sudden loud sounds, and other elements.
- Children give responses indicating a gradual shift from memory for the movement to memory for the musical events.

Follow-up

- Perform for the children a familiar song three ways, for example, sung a cappella, played on recorder, and sung with chorded-zither accompaniment. Ask children what was the same and what was different about each rendition. Explain briefly the term "arrangement," then play a recording of the original Bártok piano piece while students look at the visual previously constructed to find similarities and differences.

STANDARD 3A

Responding to music: Children identify the sources of a
wide variety of sounds.

Objective

- Children will discriminate
  aurally among various classroom percussion instruments
  and everyday objects used as
  sound sources.

Materials

- Classroom percussion instruments
- Everyday objects that may be
  used to create sounds

Prior Knowledge and Experiences

- Children have responded with
  movement to musical and verbal cues.
- Children have had exploratory
  experiences with classroom
  percussion instruments.

Procedures

1. Have a group discussion on the different ways the children like to
   move their bodies.
2. Recite each verse of the following poem for the children, encouraging them to participate in the movements. Recite poem in a rhythmic, lilting, 6/8 style.

   I like to hop, I like to hop,

   My father says, "Oh, please don't hop!"

   But all I can do is hop all day—

   Hop, hop, hop.

   I like to wiggle, I like to wiggle,

   My mother says, "Oh, please don't wiggle!"

   But all I can do is wiggle all day—

   Wiggle, wiggle, wiggle.

   I like to twist, I like to twist,

   My brother says, "Oh, please don't twist!"

   But all I can do is twist all day—

   Twist, twist, twist.

   I like to wave, I like to wave,

   My sister says, "Oh, please don't wave!"

   But all I can do is wave all day—

   Wave, wave, wave.

   I like to smile, I like to smile,

   Everyone says, "Oh, please don't smile!"

   But all I can do is smile all day—

   Smile, smile, smile.

   —*by Susan Tarnowski, used with permission*

3. Add instruments on each of the movement words. You may demonstrate this first, then invite the children to join you (for example, hop = woodblock, wiggle = flexitone or guiro, twist = ratchet or cabasa, wave = slide whistle or jingle bells, smile = triangle).

4. Collect the instruments and place them in a "music surprise box." Play each instrument out of the sight of the children, and ask them to respond with the associated movement.

Indicators of Success

- Children recognize the sounds and respond appropriately.

Follow-up

- Children create new verses for the poem and explore classroom instruments and other sound sources to accompany the new movements.

Responding to music: Children identify the sources of a
wide variety of sounds.

Objective

- Children will identify animal-
  like sounds made by the
  teacher and produce similar
  sounds.

Materials

- Pictures of farm animals
  attached to yarn to hang
  around children's necks
  (optional)

Prior Knowledge and Experiences

- Children are familiar with
  farms and farm animals and
  their sounds.

Procedures

1. Tell children a story about a farmer whose cows, horses, chickens,
   and sheep got out of their pens one night. Explain how the farmer
   found them by listening for the sounds they make. Make each animal sound and ask students to identify the animal. Let children
   practice the sounds.

2. Have each child decide which animal to pretend to be; choose at
   least one child to be the farmer. Pictures of chosen animals may be
   placed around the children's necks.

3. Have the children act out the story, establishing "pens" in which
   each group of animals lives. While the farmers pretend to sleep
   with eyes closed, the animals find a place in the classroom to hide.
   When all have hidden, awaken the farmers.

4. When the farmers call "Here, cows," all the cows must answer with
   their sound. The farmers listen to locate the sounds. They find all
   the cows and pretend to lead them back to their pen, feed them,
   and welcome them home. The activity is repeated for the remaining animals.

5. Repeat the story, allowing children to change characters.

Indicators of Success

- Children perform animal sounds and identify them aurally.

Follow-up

- Add other animals to the story.

- Change the story to one about a zookeeper and zoo animals.

- Read picture books that include animal sounds; have the children
  provide the sounds.

Responding to music: Children identify the sources of a
wide variety of sounds.

Objective

- Children will recognize that each person's singing voice is recognizable based on its own unique sound.

Materials

- "Who's That Tapping at My Window?" in *150 American Folk Songs* edited by Peter Erdei (New York: Boosey & Hawkes, 1974) and *American Folksongs for Children* by Ruth Crawford Seeger (Garden City, NY: Doubleday, 1980)

Prior Knowledge and Experiences

- The children have been in the classroom together for a few months and know each other well.
- The children know the song.

Procedures

1. Review the song.

2. Turn the song into a game. Choose one child to hide his or her eyes and listen to see who will be singing the answers to the questions. The entire class sings the first verse of the song (the questions). One child, who has been cued silently by the teacher, sings the second verse of the song (the answers). At the conclusion of the song, the child who is the listener opens his or her eyes and identifies the child who sang the solo. Continue the game with the soloist becoming the listener.

3. Discuss how the children could tell who was singing by listening to the voice. (Children may also notice that they could use the direction or distance of the sound to assist in deciding who had been singing.)

Indicators of Success

- Children identify classmates based on understanding of the unique qualities of different voices.

Follow-up

- Play similar singing games, such as "Button and Key."
- Record voices of teachers or other adults who interact regularly with the children, and play tapes for the children to figure out who is singing.

Responding to music: Children identify the sources of a wide variety of sounds.

Objective

- Children identify familiar objects used by composers as "musical instruments."

Materials

- Recording of "Pop! Goes the Weasel" by Lucien Caillet, available on *Music, USA* in the Bowmar Orchestral Library (Miami: Warner Brothers, 1994)
- Audio-playback equipment

Prior Knowledge and Experiences

- Children know the song "Pop! Goes the Weasel" from *Go in and out the Window* by Dan Fox (New York: Metropolitan Museum of Art/Henry Holt, 1987) and *The Music Connection*, Grade K (Morristown, NJ: Silver Burdett Ginn, 1995).

Procedures

1. Review the song "Pop! Goes the Weasel." Have the children sing the song replacing the word "pop" with a clap. Experiment with several other sounds.

2. Explain that a composer created special music for the song, using interesting sounds every time the song says "pop." Ask the children to listen to the song (theme and variation #1 of "Pop! Goes the Weasel" by Caillet) and see if they can figure out each sound.

3. Have the children share their responses. Listen to the song again, this time using the pause mechanism on the tape recorder to stop the music after each "pop" so that its sound source may be identified.

4. Play the complete selection once more, while the children pantomime playing the "pops" along with the recording.

Indicators of Success

- Children identify the sound sources used to produce the "pop" sounds.

Follow-up

- Place a selection of sound sources out of view of the group. Have a child choose a sound source to use for the "pop," remaining out of sight. Have the group perform the song; let the child make the pop sound; and have the group identify the sound source.

- Have the children listen to a recording of the "Toy" Symphony (attributed to Franz Joseph Haydn on some recordings, also recorded as *Cassatio ex G* or *Kindersymphonie* by Leopold Mozart) and identify the toys used as instruments, or to "The Typewriter" by Leroy Anderson to identify the actual typewriter sounds in the music.

Responding to music: Children identify the sources of a wide variety of sounds.

Objective

- Children will recognize selected classical and folk instruments by sight and sound.

Materials

- A visitor who demonstrates an actual instrument
- Audio recordings, video recordings, pictures, and picture books featuring the instrument
- Audio- and video-playback equipment

Prior Knowledge and Experiences

- Children use the word "instrument" to describe objects that produce sounds used in music.

Procedures

1. Arrange for a live demonstration of a selected instrument, by high school or college students, parents or grandparents, or community members. (Direct experience is essential for young children. If a live demonstration is impossible, however, use a video, or pictures plus audio recordings, so the visual and sound images are paired.)

2. In preparation for the demonstration, display the picture of the instrument around the room and point it out by name. If possible, read picture books featuring the instrument; for example, *Ben's Trumpet* by Rachel Isadora (New York: Greenwillow Books, 1979) or *The Old Banjo* by Stephen Gammell (New York: Aladdin, 1983).

3. At the demonstration and in subsequent discussions, ask the children to describe the sound and how the sound is made, as well as the appearance of and their impressions of the instrument.

4. Follow up with recordings or videos featuring the instrument.

Indicators of Success

- Children describe the sound and appearance of selected instruments with which they have had experience and recognize them aurally.

Follow-up

- Add new instruments to the children's experiences periodically.

- Have children play an "air instrument" (pantomime the playing action on an imaginary instrument) to accompany a recording in which the instrument is heard prominently.

Responding to music: Children respond through movement to music of various tempos, meters, dynamics, modes, genres, and styles to express what they hear and feel in works of music.

Objective

- Children will respond to music through gross motor movements, reflecting the music's style, mood, and prominent musical characteristics.

Materials

- Piano or other instrument that may be used by the teacher for improvisation

Prior Knowledge and Experiences

- Children can distinguish sound from silence and have participated in free movement.

Procedures

1. Ask the children to find their own space in the room where they are not touching anything or anybody. Establish the rules for movement: "No traffic jams or bumps or crashes," and "When the music starts, we start; and when the music stops, we stop."

2. Remind the children to move when they hear the music and freeze when it stops. Ask them to pretend that they are being watched through a big window, but the watcher can't hear the music, and their job is to show the watcher what the music sounds like by the way they move.

3. Begin improvising on the piano or other instrument (teachers not experienced with the piano can create pleasing improvisations by using only the black keys). Start with extreme contrasts of mood and style.

4. Stop playing periodically to keep the children focused on the auditory stimulation. Start the music again when all the children are still.

Indicators of Success

- Children's movements reflect the characteristics of the music.

Follow-up

- Repeat the activity with increasingly subtle or complex contrasts in the music.

Responding to music: *Children respond through movement to music of various tempos, meters, dynamics, modes, genres, and styles to express what they hear and feel in works of music.*

Objective

- Children will use their bodies and props to interpret music.

Materials

- A variety of recorded music reflecting various musical characteristics in a variety of styles (for example, Western classical music, jazz, music from nonwestern cultures, electronic music, various instruments in solos and combination)

- Audio-playback equipment that may be operated by the children

- A variety of props in a "music prop box" (for example, scarves, streamers, inflated balloons, paper fans, small stuffed animals)

Prior Knowledge and Experiences

- Children have experience creating movements to accompany songs or recorded selections.

Procedures

1. During large-group time, show the children the music prop box that will be available during their free-choice time. Demonstrate different possibilities for how the props might be used, incorporating children's suggestions.

2. Hand out props to the children. Ask the children to use the prop to help show what the music sounds like or how it makes them feel. Play a musical selection and join them as they move with their props to interpret the music.

3. Make the box available during free-play or center time, along with a cassette player and tapes so children may choose to play various selections. The teacher can model some movements while encouraging children to discover their own personal interpretations.

Indicators of Success

- Children choose to participate in the activity.

- Children's movements will reflect the general style and characteristics of the music.

Follow-up

- Switch the props and the musical selections that are available.

- Encourage children to use additional objects of their choice as props.

Responding to music: Children respond through movement to music of various tempos, meters, dynamics, modes, genres, and styles to express what they hear and feel in works of music.

Objective

- Children will demonstrate through whole body movement the sensation of gentle and light as it relates to similar qualities in a recorded example.

Materials

- Recording of "Aquarium" from *Carnival of the Animals* by Camille Saint-Saëns
- Audio-playback equipment
- Bubble solution

Prior Knowledge and Experiences

- Children have explored a variety of creative movement activities.
- Children have experience blowing bubbles with bubble solution and wands, and "catching" bubbles blown by another child or adult.

Procedures

1. Using bubble solution, blow bubbles to the children. Ask the children to let a bubble land in their hands. Turn this into a pretend activity using pantomime, asking children to catch pretend bubbles.

2. Lead the class in gently lifting their bubbles high above their heads and then tipping the bubbles so they float softly down. Have each child point with the other hand to follow the bubble as it floats down. Repeat this several times.

3. Have children insert an imaginary straw into the bubble and slowly blow the bubble larger and larger until they are able to get inside the bubble. Ask the children to gently paint the inside of their bubble.

4. Ask the children to move their bubble gently to some other place in the room, using as many different body parts as possible. Caution the children not to bump into another child's bubble because their own bubble will break, and they won't be able to finish the bubble dance.

5. Tell the children to step carefully out of the bubble, and that the bubble is getting smaller and smaller so it can be held in their hand.

6. Invite the children to lift their bubble over their heads one more time and tip the bubble, pointing with the other hand as it floats all the way down to the ground. They also might blow the bubble gently and follow as it floats away into space.

7. Lead the children to perform the bubble motions with the recording of "Aquarium" (save for later or another day if the children's attention is waning). Have the bubble float to the ground or float away during the final moments of the music.

Indicators of Success

- Children move in an appropriate manner reflecting the expressive quality of a gentle and light recorded example.

Follow-up

- Repeat activity without the teacher modeling, but rather with children creating their own movement sequence.

- Play other pieces of music, asking the children to decide which pieces sound gentle and light like "Aquarium." Listen to music that is heavy or forceful, and have the children figure out ways to move accordingly.

Responding to music: Children respond through movement to music of various tempos, meters, dynamics, modes, genres, and styles to express what they hear and feel in works of music.

Objective

- Children will move expressively and change movements in response to different sections in musical selections.

Materials

- Recording of a multisection composition or suite with very short sections, such as *Concerto Madrigal for Two Guitars and Orchestra* by Joaquín Rodrigo, *The Nutcracker Suite* by Peter I. Tchaikovsky, "Jeux d'Enfants" ("Children's Games") by Georges Bizet, *Carnival of the Animals* by Camille Saint-Saëns

Prior Knowledge and Experiences

- Children have experience with movement activities.

Procedures

1. Play one section from the piece for the children (for example, the "Pastoral" from *Concerto Madrigal),* inviting them to move their hands in some way that they choose to show how the music sounds (this focuses their attention on listening).

2. Repeat the activity, this time playing a contrasting section (for example, the "Fandango"). Ask the children to notice that the music sounded different, and point out, or have children demonstrate, that there were differences in their movements, too.

3. Tell the children that you will play one of the two sections again, to see if they can figure out which one it is (this may be presented as a game). Ask them to show their choice through their hand motions. If there are descriptive titles for each section, share these with the children (for example, games represented by sections of the "Jeux d'Enfants").

4. When the children can demonstrate that they recognize each section, invite them to create standing or moving actions to show what each one sounds like.

5. Each day or two, add another section of the piece to their repertoire, using similar procedures. Each time, repeat the previously learned sections as well. Add as many as the children's attention spans will allow, or as many as they seem to be able to remember and enjoy.

Indicators of Success

- Children will move independently and expressively, using different movements in response to the different sections of the music.

Follow-up

- Have the music available for children to use during free play time.
- Repeat at another time of the year with different pieces.
- Suggest that the children create drawings or paintings to reflect the different sections of the music.

Responding to music: Children respond through movement to music of various tempos, meters, dynamics, modes, genres, and styles to express what they hear and feel in works of music.

Objective

- Children will create movements to correlate with contrasts in the expressive characteristics of recorded musical examples (for example, dynamics, articulation, mood, tempo).

Materials

- Recording of pieces characterized by contrasting sections, for example, "Run Run" from *Memories of Childhood* by Octavio Pinto (fast/slow), available on *Classroom Concert,* Bowmar Orchestral Library (Miami: Warner Brothers, 1994), or "Javanaise" from *Suite for Flute and Jazz Piano* by Claude Bolling (bouncy/lyric)
- Audio-playback equipment

Prior Knowledge and Experiences

- Children have experience with movement activities.

Procedures

1. Play the first segment of the piece, asking children to listen and choose a movement that fits the music, one that "looks like the music sounds." Encourage them to experiment until they find a movement that pleases them.

2. Explain that the music will be played again and will keep going this time. Challenge the children to be very good listeners so that they hear when the music changes. Ask them to show the change by creating a new movement that shows what the new section sounds like. Remind them to listen carefully, because the first part may come back again, or there may be a new section, which they should show with their movement. Proceed with the activity.

3. Have the children describe what happened in the music: how many times they changed, how they moved, why they moved the way they did, and so on.

4. Repeat the activity, providing the opportunity for the children to use the same movements or to try new movements if they choose.

Indicators of Success

- Children create movements that demonstrate the expressive contrasts in the musical example and perform them at the appropriate times.

Follow-up

- Repeat the activity with different musical examples.
- Place the listening examples in the music center for individual or small-group listening and movement experiences.

Responding to music: Children participate freely in music activities.

Objective

- Children will identify picture books based on songs and will sing as they read.

Materials

- Picture books illustrating children's songs; for example, *The Farmer in the Dell* by Mary Maki Rae (New York: Viking Kestrel, 1988); *Skip to My Lou* by Nadine Bernard Westcott (Boston: Little, Brown & Company, 1989); *Mary Had a Little Lamb* by Sarah Josepha Hale (New York: Scholastic, 1990); *Oh, A-Hunting We Will Go* by John Langstaff (New York: Aladdin, 1991)

Prior Knowledge and Experiences

- Children should be able to sing songs associated with books in the classroom.

Procedures

1. Develop a reading center that includes books illustrating familiar children's songs as well as a comfortable area in which to sit. This should be separate from the rest of the classroom.

2. Sing a variety of children's songs in class, making sure to sing those that are associated with books in the reading center.

3. When introducing a "music" book in class, read it one time, providing an opportunity for the children to discuss the illustrations and the story. Then have children sing it through with you.

4. Structure time throughout the week when individual or small groups of children can go to the reading center and independently peruse the books.

Indicators of Success

- Children select the music books and sing them out loud to themselves or their friends.

- Children find other books at home or in the library that are music books and share them with the class.

- Children make up a tune to sing with nonmusic books while reciting the text.

Follow-up

- Have a child in the class be the reader/singer of a music book to the rest of the class.

- Encourage children to create new verses for songs in the books that are available, for example, adding animals not included in a picture book of "Old MacDonald," or including a police officer in "Wheels on the Bus" who might say, "Wear your seatbelt."

Responding to music: Children participate freely
in music activities.

Objective

- Children will volunteer motions to use while singing an action song.

Materials

- Song that includes actions and words, for example, "If You're Happy and You Know It" in *The Melody Book,* 2d ed., by Patricia Hackett (Englewood Cliffs, NJ: Prentice-Hall, 1992)

Prior Knowledge and Experiences

- Children have experience singing and moving to action songs.

Procedures

1. Invite the children to join you in singing an action song while doing the actions mentioned in the words. Repeat several times, changing the words and motions each time.

2. Ask the children to volunteer new movements to replace the ones in the song. They may demonstrate the movement (but also should be encouraged to use words to describe them to increase their vocabulary). For example, "clap your hands" might be replaced with "twirl around," "hug yourself," "take a bow," "wiggle your nose."

3. Repeat the song as long as there are volunteers and the children maintain interest.

Indicators of Success

- Children volunteer ideas to include in the song.

Follow-up

- Model a wide variety of interesting movements; help children explore the many ways their bodies can move.

- Repeat the activity with different songs; for example, "Clap Your Hands" and "Stamping Land."

Responding to music: Children participate freely
in music activities.

Objective

- Children will respond to music placed in their play environment.

Materials

- Portable cassette or CD player with a long, heavy-duty extension cord (or batteries)

Prior Knowledge and Experiences

- None required

Procedures

1. On occasion, take a tape player to the playground. Play lively selections of music that will be heard well outside (for example, marches, steel band, Dixieland jazz).

2. Some children will respond to the music and adapt their play to it, either by design or without consciously thinking about it. Notice the children's responses, and if appropriate point them out to other children or encourage others to join in, taking care to remain unobtrusive and not intervene to direct the children's play.

Indicators of Success

- Children's play reflects or incorporates the music in the environment.
- Children request that music be played outside during playtime.

Follow-up

- Children initiate their own musical games or accompany their play with music, sounds, and/or rhythmic movement.

*Responding to music: Children participate freely
in music activities.*

Objective

- Children will sing songs and play musical games during free time.

Materials

- Jump ropes, long bamboo poles to use as limbo sticks, paper or cloth "flags"
- A variety of playground chants, songs, and singing games
- Portable cassette or CD player and recordings (optional)

Prior Knowledge and Experiences

- Children have experience playing singing games.

Procedures

In class, teach a variety of songs and games, making sure the children can repeat them independently. Make sure all equipment necessary for these games is available during free time.

- Teach children an easy partner hand-clap pattern (for example, clap own hands, then clap partner's hands) to accompany playground chants such as "Miss Mary Mack." As children become proficient, they may create their own clapping patterns.

- Teach the children an approximation of jumping rope. Using any childhood rhyme, have children jump to the beat while chanting the rhyme. Next, have the children jump back and forth over a rope that has been stretched out on the ground. Then, hold one end of the rope while another adult or child holds the other end. Swing the rope gently in a rocking motion while children jump over it. Add the rhyme to the rope jumping when children are ready.

- Teach some calypso-style songs ("Tinga Lay-O," "Day-O") or have recordings and a cassette or CD player available. Sing the song repeatedly while doing the limbo dance. Hold a bamboo pole at one end while another adult holds the other end. Have children take turns walking or "dancing" under the stick (the actual "limbo" motion of bending backwards is too difficult for most children). After the last child has passed under, lower the stick a little bit. Keep lowering the stick until children left can no longer "dance" under the stick without touching hands to the ground.

- Visit a marching band flag corps in rehearsal, or invite some members to do a demonstration for the group. Have paper or cloth "flags" available for the children to use to create their own "routines" to recorded band music.

Indicators of Success

- Children elect to participate in musical activities on the playground.

Follow-up

- Add games and chants to the children's repertoire.
- Add props, such as "hula" hoops and batons. Invite children to use them in choreographing movements to recorded music.

Responding to music: Children participate freely in music activities.

Objective

- Children will volunteer to perform for the weekly "music shows" and will respond appropriately as performer or audience member.

Materials

- Appropriate props, instruments, or recordings

Prior Knowledge and Experiences

- Children have experience as the leader in group music or movement activities, and/or experience with individual singing in the context of singing games and activities.

Procedures

1. Explain that the class will have weekly "music shows." They are opportunities for children to present a rhyme, sing a song, play an instrument, or dance to music for their friends. Children may volunteer, with individual encouragement or assistance from the teacher as necessary. This should be kept very informal and unpressured, a variation of regular "sharing time."

2. Discuss the role of a performer (someone who has thought about and practiced his or her musical act ahead of time, stands in front of the group to perform, bows when finished).

3. Discuss what an "audience" is and define good audience behavior (listening politely, applauding at the conclusion). Have the children practice being a good audience, and praise them when they are successful.

4. Have the first show. The teacher or a parent may by the opening act to provide a model, or several adults may even put on a complete show the first week.

5. Make this a regular class activity. If there are too many volunteers for the attention span of the audience, create a schedule for taking turns, or have more than one music show per week.

Indicators of Success

- Most children volunteer to participate as a performer.
- Children demonstrate appropriate audience behavior.

Follow-up

- Discuss and/or model duets and trios, and encourage children to work together as performers.
- Invite guest performers to participate (parents, grandparents, siblings, local musicians).

Understanding music: Children use their own vocabulary and standard music vocabulary to describe voices, instruments, music notation, and music of various genres, styles, and periods from diverse cultures.

Objective

- Children will listen to pairs of short musical examples and describe or demonstrate what is the same or different about them.

Materials

- Music tape with pairs of short examples (fifteen to forty-five seconds per example) that have an obvious similarity or difference
- Cassette player

Prior Knowledge and Experiences

- Children know how to listen quietly to music.
- Children know the meanings of same and different.

Procedures

1. Construct a listening tape for use in class. Examples might include:
   - Wynton Marsalis playing a trumpet in jazz and classical styles
   - Men singing Gregorian chant and "Take Six" singing gospel
   - Drum solo from a big band recording and African drumming
   - Orchestra playing fast (Spring from Vivaldi's "Four Seasons") and orchestra playing slow ("Adagio for Strings" by Barber)
   - Rap (people speaking) and song (people singing)

   When making the tape, keep the following in mind: make each example short; use a wide variety of styles of music; place comparison pieces adjacent to each other on the tape; use the best quality recordings you can find to make the tape (CDs are best); use a total of three or four pairs per tape.

2. Play a pair of examples and ask children to describe or demonstrate with movement what is the same and what is different about the examples. Repeat their descriptions and augment them with other terms to increase their vocabulary. Listen and move again to strengthen the associations.

Indicators of Success

- Children listen attentively during the examples.
- Children find words or motions to describe similarities and differences.
- Children expand the vocabulary they use to describe music.

Follow-up

- Sing a song two different ways and ask children what was different.
- Play a longer excerpt and ask children to describe the music.

Understanding music: Children use their own vocabulary and standard music vocabulary to describe voices, instruments, music notation, and music of various genres, styles, and periods from diverse cultures.

Objective

- Children move to a piece of music and describe why they moved the way they did.

Materials

- Recordings representing a variety of styles
- Audio-playback equipment
- Large floor space for movement

Prior Knowledge and Experiences

- Children have experience moving freely to music.

Procedures

1. Have recordings available of a variety of music—marches, polkas, Dixieland, African, calypso, country, and so on.

2. Invite children to listen to the music and move the way the music sounds. Working in small groups or with individual children will result in more unique movements and verbal responses.

3. Ask children to describe what they heard that made them move the way they did, encouraging them to discuss their responses. All of the children's responses, which may range from musical descriptors ("it was fast") to imagery ("it sounded like butterflies") to judgments ("I liked it a lot") should be accepted enthusiastically. Suggest vocabulary or prompt additional responses as appropriate.

Indicators of Success

- Children move freely to music of many different styles.
- Children provide increasingly detailed descriptions of the music.

Follow-up

- Have the recordings available for children to use during free-choice time. Change the selections regularly.
- Suggest that children draw pictures while listening to music and describe why the music made them draw a particular way.

Understanding music: Children use their own vocabulary and standard music vocabulary to describe voices, instruments, music notation, and music of various genres, styles, and periods from diverse cultures.

Objective

- Children will describe the similarities and differences between songs and poems.

Materials

- *Eency Weency Spider* by Joanne Oppenheim (New York: Byron Press/Scholastic, 1991)

Prior Knowledge and Experiences

- Children can perform the finger play while singing "Eency Weency Spider."

Procedures

1. Review the song "Eency Weency Spider" while performing the finger play.

2. Sing the first few pages of the book, corresponding to the usual version of the song, while showing the pictures.

3. Stop at the page with the poetic refrain ("Oh, Eency Weency Spider, Weave your silvery web"). Ask the children to listen to the new words about Eency Weency. Read the poem and engage children in a discussion about the meaning.

4. Sing the song version again, and then read the poem. Ask the children to discuss what is different about the two versions and what is the same. When they identify the distinction between singing and speaking the words, define the difference for them as a "song" and a "poem."

5. Continue through the book, using the terminology "song" and "poem" to describe how you will present the next section; for example, "here are some new words to sing in the song"; "here is the poem again—speak some of the words with me if you know them." When the children are familiar with the book, they will be able to look at the pages and identify the poem each time it occurs.

Indicators of Success

- Children use the terms "song" and "poem" appropriately to describe examples presented to them.

Follow-up

- Lead the children in reciting short, familiar poems and songs, in no apparent order (children will figure out if the teacher is merely alternating) and have the children decide if they are poems or songs.

- Choose a nursery rhyme with a tune that the children know very well, and perform it both as a poem and as a song, so the children see how poems may be turned into songs.

- Choose a familiar poem and have the children turn it into a song by improvising a simple melody.

Understanding music: Children use their own vocabulary and standard music vocabulary to describe voices, instruments, music notation, and music of various genres, styles, and periods from diverse cultures.

Objective

- Children will label and describe the style of music according to its function (lullaby, march, and so on).

Materials

- Children's songs and recorded selections representing various functional styles of music. Lullaby examples: "Hush Little Baby," "Brahms' Lullaby," or selections from *A Child's Gift of Lullabyes* (Nashville, TN: J. Aaron Brown & Associates, 1986). March examples: "March of the Toys" from *Babes in Toyland* by Victor Herbert or various marches by John Philip Sousa
- Audio-playback equipment

Prior Knowledge and Experiences

- Children have sung songs reflecting a variety of different moods and styles.

Procedures

1. Ask the children to listen to your song and decide why someone would sing it. Sing "Hush Little Baby" in the appropriate style (slowly, softly, and sweetly). Solicit the children's responses. If necessary, help them decide that it is meant to put a baby to sleep. Have them describe why this is appropriate. Ask children if they have heard someone sing or play a lullaby to them or to a younger brother or sister.

2. Sing the song while the children pretend to rock babies in their arms.

3. Tell the children that sometimes lullabies don't use words. Play an instrumental lullaby and have them describe how it is the same or different (no words, but still soft, slow, gentle, like rocking).

4. Ask children to listen to a new piece to decide if it is a lullaby. Play a recording of a fast, spirited march. Engage children in a discussion about the music, asking questions as necessary to elicit descriptors in comparison to the lullaby (faster, louder, more exciting, makes you want to get up and move, and so forth).

5. Identify the music as a march. Ask if children have seen people march in a parade or a marching band. Explain that the march helps people all move together.

6. Play the march again while the children parade around the room, pantomiming playing instruments (children at this age should not be expected to march to the steady beat).

7. Review lullabies and marches and their characteristics.

Indicators of Success

- Children use the terms lullaby and march to label music and can describe some of their characteristics.

Follow-up

- Play and sing additional examples for the children to analyze and label. Add additional styles, such as work songs, sea songs, ballads, and waltzes.
- Sing and discuss related picture/song books, such as *Parade* by Donald Crews (New York: Mulberry, 1986) and *Once, A Lullaby* by Anita Lobel and B. P. Nichol (New York: Greenwillow, 1983).

Understanding music: Children use their own vocabulary and standard music vocabulary to describe voices, instruments, music notation, and music of various genres, styles, and periods from diverse cultures.

Objective

- Children will begin to recognize that music has its own symbol system.

Materials

- A picture book based on a song that has the music notation printed in the book and/or illustrated songbooks such as *Go in and out the Window* by Dan Fox (New York: Metropolitan Museum of Art/Henry Holt, 1987) or *Shake It to the One That You Love Best* by Cheryl Warren Mattox (El Sabrante, CA: Warren-Mattox Productions, 1989)

- Paper with the melodies of simple, familiar songs printed on the bottom in music notation.

- Crayons, markers, or paints

Prior Knowledge and Experiences

- Children are beginning to recognize that words and numbers are symbols of language.

- Children have noticed the music notation for songs in songbooks and picture books of songs.

Procedures

1. Choose a picture book based on a song that includes a page showing the music notation. "Sing" the book with the class. At the end, point out the musical notes as "the special way we write music."

2. Sing several familiar songs from an illustrated songbook while holding the pages up so the children can see them. Ask the children to discuss what they see on the page. In addition to the music, they should notice the art work. Place the songbooks in a music or book center where the children may access them.

3. As a small-group or individual activity, provide children with one of the pages with the music notation printed at the bottom. Tell them what the song is and sing it with them. Invite them to provide a picture or design to illustrate the page of music, like the songbooks they have already worked with.

4. Invite children to hold up their song pages, one at a time, during group singing time, so all of the children can view and sing the illustrated song.

Indicators of Success

- Children can point out music notation and label it "written music," "music written down," or something similar.

Follow-up

- Periodically add new song pages for the children to illustrate.

- Make large staff lines on paper and models of simple music symbols available for free-choice time, so children who are interested may experiment with writing/copying music notation in the same way they experiment with writing/copying letters and numbers.

Understanding music: Children sing, play instruments, move, or verbalize to demonstrate awareness of the elements of music and changes in their usage.

Objective

- Children will perform different tempos and gradually change tempos in singing and movement.

Materials

- Familiar song that describes an action, such as "Row, Row, Row Your Boat"

Prior Knowledge and Experiences

- The children know the song.

Procedures

1. Have the children sing a familiar song that describes an action. Use a moderate tempo. Have the children pretend to be making the corresponding motions (for example, rowing) while singing.

2. Make up a story with events that have different speeds (slow, fast, slowing down, and speeding up) and have the children sing the song and move accordingly. For example, you might say, "You have been rowing for such a long time that you are getting very tired, and your rowing is getting slower and slower," and then sing the song several times, each time a little more slowly; have the children perform the rowing motions accordingly. Or, you could say, "It is starting to get dark, so you'd better row very quickly to get to shore," and then sing the song at a fast tempo several times while the children "row" along.

3. Encourage children to make up stories that include events that are fast, slow, speeding up, and slowing down. Have them demonstrate the corresponding movements while singing.

Indicators of Success

- Children demonstrate the different tempos and gradually changing tempos in their singing and movement.

Follow-up

- Use similar activities, varying the songs, movements, and musical elements.

- Play recordings of music with clear tempo changes and have the children move to show the changes.

Understanding music: Children sing, play instruments, move, or verbalize to demonstrate awareness of the elements of music and changes in their usage.

Objective

- Children will perform gradual changes in dynamics; for example, crescendo (gradually getting louder) and decrescendo (gradually getting softer).

Materials

- An object to be used in a hide-and-seek type game
- Hand drum with beater

Prior Knowledge and Experiences

- Children can perform music that is loud and soft and recognize these characteristics aurally.

Procedures

1. In full view of the children, hide the object in the room. Ask the children to figure out when the hand drum (played with a beater) gets louder and when it get softer. Play loudly near the object, and get gradually softer while walking away from the object, until you are on the other side of the room and playing very softly; then reverse the process to return to the object. Discuss the process and help the children identify the relationship between the sound and distance.

2. Turn the activity into a game. Choose a searcher to wait with eyes closed while a hider hides the object. Have the searcher move slowly around the room to look for the object. The other children (or one child) give clues as to where the object is hidden: they must watch the searcher and continuously patsch (pat their knees), play the drum, or chant a steady beat or rhythm pattern softly or loudly. Instruct them to gradually change the dynamics depending on how close or far the searcher is to the hidden object. The searcher follows the dynamic clues to find the object.

Indicators of Success

- Children successfully provide the crescendos and decrescendos as clues, and respond to the clues to find the object.

Follow-up

- Play a similar game using the song "I've Lost the Closet Key" in *150 American Folk Songs* edited by Peter Erdei (New York: Boosey & Hawkes, 1974).

- Sing songs and create sound pieces using crescendo and decrescendo.

Understanding music: Children sing, play instruments, move, or verbalize to demonstrate awareness of the elements of music and changes in their usage.

Objective

- Children will recognize and respond to repeated rhythm patterns (for example, short-short-long) found in many traditional children's songs.

Materials

- Songs with a repeated, obvious rhythm pattern; for example, the "short, short, long" (SSL) pattern found in "Mary Had a Little Lamb" ("lit-tle lamb"), "Wheels on the Bus" ("'round and 'round"), "Six Little Ducks" ("quack, quack, quack"), "London Bridge" ("fal-ling down"), "Are You Sleeping" ("Bro-ther John" and "ding, ding, dong")

Prior Knowledge and Experiences

- None required

Procedures

1. Sing one of the songs, demonstrating an action during the SSL pattern. Example: stroking one forearm with the opposite hand like petting a lamb during "Mary Had a Little Lamb." (Clapping is not recommended because it does not reinforce the length of the sound, but rather the length of the silence between claps.)

2. Have the children imitate the motion while you sing the song again. Reinforce the children and introduce the terminology by pointing out how well "you are moving short, short, long with me." Have the children speak and do the movement to the words "short, short, looong" (holding out the vowel to create the appropriate duration for the word "long"). If a child is having difficulty, the teacher can stroke the child's arm so he or she feels the sensations of the pattern.

3. Repeat the song until children can perform the movement independently.

4. Introduce a new song, challenging the children to find the pattern and to create a corresponding motion.

Indicators of Success

- Children respond to the rhythm pattern independently by moving.
- Children recognize the same pattern in different songs.

Follow-up

- As children find or learn additional SSL songs, put them on a chart, or make pages for each song that children can illustrate to create a songbook.

- Associate visual icons or Cuisenaire Rods of the appropriate lengths with the sounds, and have the children use them to experiment by arranging them in different and longer patterns.

- Identify other common rhythm patterns that the children will be able to recognize and respond to; for example, "short, short, short, short, long," as in "This Old Man" ("give the dog a bone") and "Old MacDonald" ("ee-i-ee-i-oh").

Understanding music: Children sing, play instruments, move, or verbalize to demonstrate awareness of the elements of music and changes in their usage.

Objective

- Children will differentiate between music played in low and high registers.

Materials

- Recording of "Placidly" from *Five Preludes* by William Grant Still

- Audio-playback equipment

Prior Knowledge and Experiences

- Children have used their voices to explore high and low sounds.

Procedures

1. Have the children stretch up high while making a high, hooty sound like an owl. Have them reach down low, making a low sound like a whale. Switch back and forth several times to be sure the children understand the relationships.

2. Tell the children they will hear high and low sounds played by a piano in the recording you will play for them. Ask them to show you with their movements when they are hearing the high and low sounds. Play the recording of "Placidly," helping them to discover that the music is structured into patterns of low, high, high (if necessary, provide assistance by modeling the appropriate movements).

3. Repeat the activity, asking children to keep their eyes closed. (This way the teacher can judge whether the children are responding individually, without imitating peers.)

4. Discuss the pattern created by the low and high sounds and the mood created by the music.

Indicators of Success

- Children's movements demonstrate discrimination between sounds performed in low and high registers.

Follow-up

- Have children explore a keyboard to find where the low and high sounds are located.

- Provide opportunities for children to create low/high pieces on a keyboard or bells, while other children listen and move along.

Understanding music: Children sing, play instruments, move, or verbalize to demonstrate awareness of the elements of music and changes in their usage.

Objective

- Children will listen attentively and respond to the prominent patterns and characteristics in recorded music through movement.

Materials

- Recording of "March" from *The Comedians,* Opus 26, by Dmitri Kabelevsky
- Audio-playback equipment

Prior Knowledge and Experiences

- Children are familiar with circus clowns through actual experience or in pictures and stories.

Procedures

1. Lead children in a discussion about clowns and how they move. Tell children that they will be listening to a piece of music that has certain places where it sounds like the clowns are flopping to the ground. With children still seated, practice lifting hands over heads and then flopping over and bending at the waist down to the floor.

2. Add a descending glissando with voices or slide whistle to create the sound effects for the movement.

3. Ask children to listen carefully for the places in the music that make the clowns flop down (the three-part segment consisting of two glissandos and a slower, descending pitch pattern, which recurs several times throughout the short piece), and to show those places by doing the movement.

4. Have children demonstrate how clowns might move their arms and hands around in the air when walking. While they are still seated, have children move their "clown arms" to the music, as well as listen and respond to the descending "floppy" patterns as above.

5. Once children can respond to the musical cues independently, have them demonstrate how clowns might walk. Ask them to walk around the room like clowns, while listening carefully to show the "floppy" pattern every time they hear it. Remind them that there are lots of different kinds of clowns, each moving in different ways, to encourage creativity and individuality in their movements.

Indicators of Success

- Children listen attentively while moving, responding appropriately to the musical cues, and creating expressive, original motions to imitate the clowns.

Follow-up

- Use other sections of *The Comedians* for expressive and creative-movement activities, or for movement or dramatic play based on the circus theme.

Understanding music: Children demonstrate an awareness of music as a part of daily life.

Objective

- Children will use music to assist with their daily routines.

Materials

- Songs to use or adapt for different daily activities, for example, "Put Your Finger in the Air" in *Music: A Way of Life for the Young Child* by Kathleen Bayless and Marjorie Ramsey (Columbus, OH: Merrill, 1987) and *The Music Connection,* Grade K (Morristown, NJ: Silver Burdett Ginn, 1995)

Prior Knowledge and Experiences

- Children have experience with action songs.

Procedures

1. Contribute to the children's awareness of music as a part of daily life by creating songs in the classroom to help move children through transition times and at other times during the day. For example, during the transition process from a table art activity to group time on the floor, you might sing these words to the tune of "Put Your Finger in the Air":

   > Put your bottom on the rug, on the rug,
   >
   > Put your bottom on the rug, on the rug,
   >
   > Put your bottom on the rug, or I'll feed you great big bugs,
   >
   > Put your bottom on the rug, on the rug.

   Modeling the comfortable use of music is essential to teaching children the value of music in everyday life. (Children appreciate rhymes and silliness on the teacher's part and listen more carefully as a result.)

Indicators of Success

- Children listen to the musical cues and move effectively to their next activity.
- Children join in the songs after a few teacher repetitions.

Follow-up

- Encourage children to contribute their ideas for songs or words to use at different times or for different routines in the classroom.

Understanding music: Children demonstrate an awareness of music as a part of daily life.

Objective

- Children will become familiar with music as a medium for changing feelings.

Materials

- Recording of "Whistle a Happy Tune" from *The King & I* by Richard Rodgers and Oscar Hammerstein II
- Audio-playback equipment

Prior Knowledge and Experiences

- Children have sung songs that describe feelings, such as "If You're Happy and You Know It."

Procedures

1. Have the children listen to the song "Whistle a Happy Tune" and discuss the feelings described (fear). Have them determine how the singer used music to change her feelings from "afraid" to "not afraid."

2. Provide the children the opportunity to share experiences in their own lives when they were afraid and how they handled those situations.

3. Discuss how thinking positive thoughts or singing a happy song may help bring strong feelings such as fear or sadness under control. Have the children share happy songs they might sing to do this.

4. Discuss their ideas for other ways music may be used to change moods or make people feel better (singing to a sick friend, singing to welcome a new child in the class, and so forth).

Indicators of Success

- Children describe ways music may be used to change mood.

Follow-up

- Use music during rest time and discuss how it helps to create a calm, restful mood.

- Discuss or read stories where characters have found constructive ways to deal with fearful situations; for example, singing a song, holding someone's hand, or taking along a favorite toy, book, or blanket.

Understanding music: Children demonstrate an awareness of music as a part of daily life.

Objective

- Children will recognize that adults who are important to them value music.

Materials

- A letter to parents explaining the activity
- Cassette recorders or video recorders the children or parents can operate (optional)

Prior Knowledge and Experiences

- Children can identify music and music activities they enjoy.

Procedures

1. Demonstrate that music is a pleasurable activity in your life by telling children about concerts attended, playing recordings of favorite pieces for them, playing instruments for them if possible, and expressing pleasure and enthusiasm about classroom music activities and children's music making.

2. Have children become "music news reporters" and interview parents, grandparents, other adults, or siblings about what music and musical activities they enjoy or enjoyed when they were younger. Clue in the parents via a letter sent home so they can assist. If possible, encourage the children to tape their interviews, or ask parents to write down some of the answers to send with the child.

3. Have children report back on what they learn. Parts of recordings can be played for the class, or key statements may be edited onto a master tape.

Indicators of Success

- Children identify many ways through which people who are important to them enjoy music.

Follow-up

- When children have each reported on their interviews, create a group "news report" summarizing the responses. If a video recorder is available, use it to record the report so you can play it back for the class and parents.

Understanding music: Children demonstrate an
awareness of music as a part of daily life.

Objective

- Children recognize that music is found throughout the community.

Materials

- Prior arrangements with the people at the selected destinations
- Camera

Prior Knowledge and Experiences

- Children have experience singing songs or listening to music at various times, and with various purposes, throughout the day (celebrating birthdays, playing singing games, listening for relaxation at rest time).

Procedures

1. Take the children on trips to places in the community where they will find people using or making music; for example, a place of worship where there is an organist, choir, or bell choir practicing; an aerobics studio; children's dance classes; school band or choir rehearsals; rehearsal for a musical; music store; radio station; dentist's office; grocery store.

2. At each location, have the children notice what music they are hearing and how it is being used. Engage the children in a discussion with the people involved in making or playing the music about why music is important in what they do. Take photographs of the site, the people they spoke with, the instrument, and so on.

3. Create a poster or scrapbook with the photographs. Discuss and "revisit" the trip, using the photos as a stimulus. Discuss the important role music plays in many people's lives and activities, and see if the children can provide additional examples (people singing in the car or shower or dancing to music at a wedding).

Indicators of Success

- Children identify a variety of the ways music is used in people's lives.

Follow-up

- Add photos to the poster or pages to the scrapbook as new opportunities arise.
- Encourage children to cut out photos of music making from old magazines (with permission) to make a collage.

Understanding music: Children demonstrate an awareness of music as a part of daily life.

Objective

- Children will pretend to be people whose occupations are centered around music.

Materials

- A variety of props
- Cassette player with tapes that are clearly marked as to musical content

Prior Knowledge and Experiences

- Children have discussed occupations centered around music (professional musician, conductor, dancer).

Procedures

1. Design a music center around various occupations centered around music. Some examples:

   - Performing musician (include replicas or children's versions of various instruments, a microphone for singers, appropriate costumes). Music tape might include interesting pieces played by the various instruments available. Make an effort to include contrasting styles of music. Include a tape for each instrument with a picture on it for easy identification.

   - Orchestra or band director (include a conductor's baton, a wire music stand, some sheet music as a score, some stuffed animals to be ensemble members, a tuxedo T-shirt, a small podium). Music tape might include some Sousa marches, *Carnival of the Animals,* or other multimovement pieces that have short, musically contrasting sections.

   - Ballet dancer (include costumes, a large mirror, large clear space, makeup, ballet slippers, pictures of male and female ballet dancers on the wall). Music tape might include selections from the *Nutcracker Suite* or *Swan Lake.*

2. Structure time throughout the week when individual children or small groups can play in the music center.

Indicators of Success

- Children select the music center and interact with the music.
- Children recognize various occupations in music in another context such as on television.
- Parents indicate that children have been emulating musicians at home.

Follow-up

- Take children to a concert or ballet.

- Put on a program in which children have the opportunity to perform in their favorite roles.

- Read books that include characters with musical occupations; for example, *The Philharmonic Gets Dressed* by Karla Kuskin and Marc Simont (New York: Harper & Row, 1982); *Song and Dance Man* by Karen Ackerman (New York: Scholastic, 1988); *Berlioz the Bear* by Jan Brett (New York: Scholastic, 1991). Also, use books that tell stories of ballet; for example, *The Nutcracker Ballet* by Deborah Hautzig (New York: Random House, 1992); *Swan Lake* by Rachel Isadora (New York: G. P. Putnam's Sons, 1991).

OPPORTUNITY-TO-LEARN STANDARDS

For Prekindergarten and Kindergarten (ages 2–5)

Curriculum and Scheduling

1. Music is integrated into the curriculum throughout the day.

2. The children's learning experiences include singing, playing instruments, listening to music, creating music, and moving to music.

3. At least 12 percent of the contact time with children in every prekindergarten and kindergarten is devoted to experiences with music.

Staffing

1. Music instruction in every prekindergarten and kindergarten is provided by teachers who have received formal training in early-childhood music. A music specialist qualified in early-childhood education is available as a consultant.

Materials and Equipment

1. Every room in which music is taught is equipped with a high-quality sound reproduction system capable of utilizing current recording technology. At least some of the audio equipment can be operated by the children. Every teacher has convenient access to sound recordings representing a wide variety of music styles and cultures. Also available for use in music instruction are video cameras, color monitors, stereo VCRs, and multimedia equipment combining digitized sound and music with graphics and text.

2. Every room in which music is taught is equipped with a variety of classroom instruments, including drums, rhythm sticks, finger cymbals, triangles, cymbals, gongs, jingle bells, resonator bells, step bells, xylophone-type instruments with removable bars, chorded zithers, fretted instruments, electronic keyboard instruments, and assorted instruments representing a variety of cultures. Adaptive devices (e.g., adaptive picks, beaters, bells) are available for use by children with disabilities.

3. Every room in which music is taught is equipped with children's books containing songs and with other instructional materials in music.

Facilities

1. Every prekindergarten and kindergarten has a "music center" or similar area where children have easy access to music materials and can listen to music with headphones so as not to disturb others.

2. Every prekindergarten and kindergarten has an uncluttered area large enough to accommodate the largest group of children taught and to provide ample space for creative and structured movement activities.

From *Opportunity to Learn Standards for Music Instruction: Grades PreK–12.* Reston, VA: MENC, 1994.

MENC POSITION STATEMENT
ON EARLY CHILDHOOD EDUCATION

Introduction

Music is a natural and important part of young children's growth and development. Early interaction with music positively affects the quality of all children's lives. Successful experiences in music help all children bond emotionally and intellectually with others through creative expression in song, rhythmic movement, and listening experiences. Music in early childhood creates a foundation upon which future music learning is built. These experiences should be integrated within the daily routine and play of children. In this way, enduring attitudes regarding the joy of music making and sharing are developed.

Music education for young children involves a developmentally appropriate program of singing, moving, listening, creating, playing instruments, and responding to visual and verbal representations of sound. The content of such a program should represent music of various cultures in time and place. Time should be made available during the day for activities in which music is the primary focus of attention for its own value. It may also serve as a means for teachers to facilitate the accomplishment of nonmusical goals.

Musical experiences should be play-based and planned for various types of learning opportunities such as one-on-one, choice time, integration with other areas of the curriculum, and large-group music focus. The best possible musical models and activities should be provided. Adults responsible for guiding these experiences may range from parent, to caregiver, to early childhood educator, to music specialist. Music educators are committed to working in partnership with these adults to provide exemplary music experiences for young children.

Early Childhood Education

Early education for prekindergarten children in our country is provided in a variety of settings. These children represent increasingly diverse backgrounds, experiences, and risk factors, and reflect a wide range of special needs. Settings include day and family care centers, preschool, and Head Start. Public schools also sponsor prekindergarten and early intervention programs supported through federal, state, and local funding.

The music component is integral to all such programs. It serves the expressive, emotional, intellectual, social, and creative needs of all children. Music educators should take the initiative to network with parents and early childhood professionals to disseminate developmentally appropriate materials and techniques for use in curriculum planning.

A Music Curriculum for Young Children

A music curriculum for young children should include many opportunities to explore sound through singing, moving, listening, and playing instruments, as well as introductory experiences with verbalization and visualization of musical ideas. The music literature included in the curriculum should be of high quality and lasting value, including traditional children's songs, folk songs, classical music, and music from a variety of cultures, styles, and time periods.

Beliefs about Young Children and Developmentally and Individually Appropriate Musical Experiences

1. *All children have musical potential.* Every child has the potential for successful, meaningful interactions with music. The development of this potential, through numerous encounters with a wide variety of music and abundant opportunities to participate regularly in developmentally appropriate music activities, is the right of every young child.

2. *Children bring their own unique interest and abilities to the music learning environment.* Each child will take away that bit of knowledge and skill that he or she is uniquely capable of understanding and developing. Children must be left, as much as possible, in control of their own learning. They should be provided with a rich environment that offers many possible routes for them to explore as they grow in awareness and curiosity about music.

3. *Very young children are capable of developing critical thinking skills through musical ideas.* Children use thinking skills when making musical judgments and choices.

4. *Children come to early childhood music experiences from diverse backgrounds.* Their home languages and cultures are to be valued and seen as attributes that enrich everyone in the learning environment.

5. *Children should experience exemplary musical sounds, activities, and materials.* Children's learning time is valuable and should not be

wasted on experiences with music or activities of trite or questionable quality.

6. *Children should not be encumbered with the need to meet performance goals.* Opportunities should be available for children to develop accurate singing, rhythmic responses to music, and performance skills on instruments. Each child's attainment of a predetermined performance level, however, is neither essential nor appropriate.

7. *Children's play is their work.* Children should have opportunities for individual musical play, such as in a "music corner," as well as for group musical play, such as singing games. Children learn within a playful environment. Play provides a safe place to try on the roles of others, to fantasize, and to explore new ideas. Children's play involves imitation and improvisation.

8. *Children learn best in pleasant physical and social environments.* Music learning contexts will be most effective when they include (1) play, (2) games, (3) conversations, (4) pictorial imagination, (5) stories, (6) shared reflections on life events and family activities, and (7) personal and group involvement in social tasks. Dominant use of drill-type activities and exercises and worksheet tasks will not provide the kind of active, manipulative, and creative musical environment essential to the development of young minds.

9. *Diverse learning environments are needed to serve the developmental needs of many individual children.* Children interact with musical materials in their own way based on their unique experiences and developmental stages. One child may display sophistication and confidence in creating songs in response to dolls. Another child, in the same setting, may move the dolls around without uttering a sound—but this "silent participator" leaves the area content in having shared the music play. The silent participator often is later heard playing in another area softly singing to a different set of dolls—demonstrating a delayed response.

10. *Children need effective adult models.* Parents and teachers who provide music in their child's life are creating the most powerful route to the child's successful involvement in the art.

The Music Teachers of Young Children

It is desirable that individuals with training in early childhood music education for young children be involved in providing musical experiences for the children, either directly or as consultants. Often it is the parent, certified teacher, higher education professional, Child Development Associate (CDA), or other care provider who is primarily responsible for guiding the musical experiences of the young child. These persons should

- love and respect young children,

- value music and recognize that an early introduction to music is important in the lives of children,

- model an interest in and use of music in daily life,

- be confident in their own musicianship, realizing that within the many facets of musical interaction there are many effective ways to personally affect children's musical growth,

- be willing to enrich and seek improvement of personal musical and communicative skills,

- interact with children and music in a playful manner

- use developmentally appropriate musical materials and teaching techniques,

- find, create, and/or seek assistance in acquiring and using appropriate music resources,

- cause appropriate music learning environments to be created,

- be sensitive and flexible when children's interests are diverted from an original plan.

Coda

The Music Educators National Conference is committed to the implementation of this position statement. This goal can best be accomplished through the combined efforts of parents, music educators, and early childhood professionals. MENC supports policies and efforts that will make it possible for all children to participate in developmentally and individually appropriate practice in early childhood music education.

This formal position statement was developed as part of MENC's "Future Directions" effort to bring members' recommendations into reality. It was adopted by the MENC National Executive Board in July 1991. The statement was developed as a service to the profession and may be reprinted.

RESOURCES

Sources of Songs Used in This Text

Chosky, Lois. *The Kodály Method.* 2d ed. Englewood Cliffs, NJ: Prentice-Hall, 1988.

Erdei, Peter, ed. *150 American Folk Songs* New York: Boosey & Hawkes, 1974.

Feierabend, John. *Music for Little People.* New York: Boosey & Hawkes, 1989.

Feierabend, John. *Music for Very Little People.* New York: Boosey & Hawkes, 1986.

Fox, Dan. *Go in and out the Window.* New York: Metropolitan Museum of Art/Henry Holt, 1987.

Hackett, Patricia. *The Melody Book.* 2d ed. Englewood Cliffs, NJ: Prentice-Hall, 1992.

Mattox, Cheryl Warren. *Shake It to the One That You Love Best.* El Sabrante, CA: Warren-Mattox Productions, 1989.

The Music Connection. Grade K. Morristown, NJ: Silver Burdett Ginn, 1995.

The Music Connection. Grade 1. Morristown, NJ: Silver Burdett Ginn, 1995.

Seeger, Ruth Crawford. *American Folksongs for Children.* Garden City, NY: Doubleday, 1980.

Share the Music. Grade K. New York: Macmillan/McGraw-Hill, 1995.

Wirth, Marian, Verna Stassevitch, Rita Shotwell, and Patricia Stemmler. *Musical Games, Finger Plays, and Rhythmic Activities for Early Childhood.* West Nyack, NY: Parker, 1983.

Children's Books Referenced in This Text

Ackerman, Karen. *Song and Dance Man.* New York: Scholastic, 1988.

Aliki. *Corn Is Maize.* New York: Crowell, 1976.

Brett, Jan. *Berlioz the Bear.* New York: Scholastic, 1991.

Crews, Donald. *Parade.* New York: Mulberry, 1986.

Gammell, Stephen. *The Old Banjo.* New York: Aladdin, 1983.

Galdone, Paul. *The Gingerbread Man.* New York: Seabury, 1975.

Hale, Sarah Josepha. *Mary Had a Little Lamb.* New York: Scholastic, 1990.

Hamilton, Virginia, ed. *The People Could Fly.* New York: Alfred A. Knopf, 1985.

Hautzig, Deborah. *The Nutcracker Ballet.* New York: Random House, 1992.

Isadora, Rachel. *Ben's Trumpet.* New York: Greenwillow, 1979.

Isadora, Rachel. *Swan Lake.* New York: G. P. Putnam's Sons, 1991.

Jones, Carol. *This Old Man.* Boston: Houghton Mifflin, 1990.

Kuskin, Karla, and Marc Simont. *The Philharmonic Gets Dressed.* New York: Harper & Row, 1982.

Langstaff, John. *Oh, A-Hunting We Will Go.* New York: Aladdin, 1991.

Lemieux, Michelle. *Peter and the Wolf.* New York: Morrow Junior Books, 1991.

Lester, Helen. *Tacky the Penguin.* Boston: Houghton Mifflin, 1988.

Lobel, Anita, and B. P. Nichol. *Once, A Lullaby.* New York: Greenwillow, 1983.

Martin Jr., Bill. *Listen to the Rain.* New York: Henry Holt, 1988.

Munsch, Robert. *Mortimer.* Toronto: Annick, 1985.

Oppenheim, Joanne. *Eency Weency Spider.* New York: Byron Press/Scholastic, 1991.

Pellowski, Ann. *The Story Vine.* New York: Macmillan, 1984.

Prokofiev, Sergey, Maria Carlson, and Charles Mikolaycak. *Peter and the Wolf.* New York: Puffin, 1982.

Prokofiev, Sergey, and Josef Palecek. *Peter and the Wolf.* Natick, MA: Picture Book Studio, 1987.

Rae, Mary Maki. *The Farmer in the Dell.* New York: Viking Kestrel, 1988.

Shannon, George, Jose Aruego, and Ariene Dewey. *Lizard's Song.* New York: Greenwillow, 1981.

Showers, Paul. *The Listening Walk.* New York: HarperTrophy, 1991.

Silverstein, Shel. *A Light in the Attic.* New York: Harper & Row, 1981.

Westcott, Nadine Bernard. *Skip to My Lou.* Boston: Little, Brown & Company, 1989.

Wood, Audrey. *Silly Sally.* San Diego: Harcourt Brace Jovanovich, 1993.

Listening Selections Used in This Text

A Child's Gift of Lullabyes (Nashville, TN: J. Aaron Brown & Associates, 1986).

American folksong. "Hush, Little Baby."

Bach, J. S. "Air on a G String."

Bártok, Béla. "From the Diary of a Fly" (arrangement by Greene String Quartet).

Bizet, Georges. "Jeux d'Enfants" ("Children's Games").

Bolling, Claude. "Javanaise" from *Suite for Flute and Jazz Piano.*

"Brahms' Lullaby."

Caillet, Lucien. "Pop! Goes the Weasel," on *Music, USA* in the Bowmar Orchestral Library (Miami: Warner Brothers, 1994).

Herbert, Victor. "March of the Toys" from *Babes in Toyland.*

Kabelevsky, Dmitri. "March" from *The Comedians,* Opus 26.

Mussorgsky, Modeste. "Ballet of the Unhatched Chicks" from *Pictures at an Exhibition.*

Pinto, Octavio. "Run Run" from *Memories of Childhood,* on *Classroom Concert* in the Bowmar Orchestral Library (Miami: Warner Brothers, 1994).

Prokofiev, Sergey. *Peter and the Wolf.*

Rodgers, Richard, and Oscar Hammerstein II. "Whistle a Happy Tune" from *The King & I.*

Rodrigo, Joaquín. *Concerto Madrigal for Two Guitars and Orchestra.*

Saint-Saëns, Camille. *Carnival of the Animals.*

Still, William Grant. "Placidly" from *Five Preludes.*

Tchaikovsky, Peter I. *The Nutcracker Suite.*

Villa-Lobos, Hector. "The Little Train of Caipira" from *Bachianas Brasileiras.*

Teaching Methods and Curriculum Resources

*Andress, Barbara. *Promising Practices: Prekindergarten Music Education.* Reston, VA: Music Educators National Conference, 1989. #1498.

*Andress, Barbara, and Linda Walker, eds. *Readings in Early Childhood Music Education.* Reston, VA: Music Educators National Conference, 1992. #1043.

Bayless, Kathleen, and Marjorie Ramsey. *Music: A Way of Life for the Young Child.* Columbus, OH: Merrill, 1987.

Boswell, Jackie. *The Young Child and Music: Contemporary Principles in Child Development and Music Education.* Reston, VA: Music Educators National Conference, 1985.

Burton, Stephanie. *Music Explosion: Introducing Themes with Music.* Logan, IA: Perfection Learning, 1994.

Campbell, Patricia Shehan, and Carol Scott-Kassner. *Music in Childhood from Preschool through the Elementary Grades.* New York: Schirmer, 1995.

*Feierabend, John. *TIPS: Musical Activities in Early Childhood.* Reston, VA: Music Educators National Conference, 1990. #1097.

Forrai, Katalin. *Music in Preschool.* Budapest: Corvina Press, 1988.

McDonald, Dorothy, and Gene Simons. *Musical Growth and Development: Birth through Six.* New York: Schirmer Books, 1989.

*Music Educators National Conference. *Sing! Move! Listen! Music and Young Children.* Reston, VA: Music Educators National Conference, 1993. Videocassette. #3081.

*Palmer, Mary, and Wendy Sims. *Music in Prekindergarten: Planning and Teaching.* Reston, VA: Music Educators National Conference, 1993. #1031.

Reilly, Mary Louise, and Lynn Freeman Olson. *It's Time for Music.* Van Nuys, CA: Alfred, 1985.

Wood, Donna. *Move, Sing, Listen, Play.* 2d ed. Toronto: Gordon V. Thompson, 1994.

*Available from MENC.

MENC Resources on Music and Arts Education Standards

Implementing the Arts Education Standards. Set of five brochures: "What School Boards Can Do," "What School Administrators Can Do," " What State Education Agencies Can Do," "What Parents Can Do," "What the Arts Community Can Do." 1994. #4022. Each brochure is also available in packs of 20.

National Standards for Arts Education: What Every Young American Should Know and Be Able to Do in the Arts. 1994. #1605.

Opportunity-to-Learn Standards for Music Instruction: Grades PreK–12. 1994. #1619.

Perspectives on Implementation: Arts Education Standards for America's Students. 1994. #1622

Prekindergarten Music Education Standards. Brochure. 1995. #4015 (set of ten).

The School Music Program—a New Vision: The K–12 National Standards, PreK Standards, and What They Mean to Music Educators. 1994. #1618.

Teaching Examples: Ideas for Music Educators. 1994. #1620.

MENC's *Strategies for Teaching* Series

Strategies for Teaching Prekindergarten Music, compiled and edited by Wendy L. Sims. #1644.

Strategies for Teaching K–4 General Music, compiled and edited by Sandra L. Stauffer and Jennifer Davidson. #1645.

Strategies for Teaching Middle-Level General Music, compiled and edited by June M. Hinckley and Suzanne M. Shull. #1646.

Strategies for Teaching High School General Music, compiled and edited by Keith P. Thompson and Gloria J. Kiester. #1647.

Strategies for Teaching Elementary and Middle-Level Chorus, compiled and edited by Ann Roberts Small and Judy K. Bowers. #1648.

Strategies for Teaching High School Chorus, compiled and edited by Randal Swiggum. #1649.

Strategies for Teaching Strings and Orchestra, compiled and edited by Dorothy A. Straub, Louis S. Bergonzi, and Anne C. Witt. #1652.

Strategies for Teaching Middle-Level and High School Keyboard, compiled and edited by Martha F. Hilley and Tommie Pardue. #1655.

Strategies for Teaching Beginning and Intermediate Band, compiled and edited by Edward J. Kvet and Janet M. Tweed. #1650.

Strategies for Teaching High School Band, compiled and edited by Edward J. Kvet and John E. Williamson. #1651.

Strategies for Teaching Specialized Ensembles, compiled and edited by Robert A. Cutietta. #1653.

Strategies for Teaching Middle-Level and High School Guitar, compiled and edited by William E. Purse, James L. Jordan, and Nancy Marsters. #1654.

Strategies for Teaching: Guide for Music Methods Classes, compiled and edited by Louis O. Hall with Nancy R. Boone, John Grashel, and Rosemary C. Watkins. #1656.

Strategies for Teaching Technology, compiled and edited by Sam Reese, Kimberly McCord, and Kimberly Walls. #1657.

For more information on these and other MENC publications, write to or call MENC Publications Sales, 1806 Robert Fulton Drive, Reston, VA 20191-4348; 800-828-0229; or see the MENC web site (http://www.menc.org).